good deeds

good deeds

TRUE STORIES OF GOOD DEEDS,
CHARITABLE ACTS, AND SELFLESS SERVICE

DESERET
BOOK

SALT LAKE CITY, UTAH

We acknowledge copyright holders whose stories we may have included but with whom we were unable to make personal contact. All other copyrighted works are used by permission or are in public domain. If any acknowledgments have been overlooked, please notify the publisher and omissions will be rectified in future editions.

Library of Congress Cataloging-in-Publication Data

Good deeds.
   p.   cm.
   ISBN 1-57008-912-4 (pbk.)
   1. Charity.   I. Deseret Book Company.

BV4639.G667   2003
241'.4—dc21   2003004919

Printed in the United States of America   18961-7032
R. R. Donnelley and Sons, Crawfordsville, IN

10 9 8 7 6 5 4 3 2 1

Contents

contents

contents

contents

contents

x

Thanks to the following, whose efforts helped make this book possible:

Director of Publishing, Deseret Book Company
Cory H. Maxwell

Assistant Director of Publishing
Jana S. Erickson

Senior Editor
Jay A. Parry

Compiler and Editor
Lisa Mangum

Research Assistant
Dennis Gaunt

Graphic Designer
Sheryl Dickert

Typography
Kent R. Minson

Proofreaders
Amy Felix
Linda Gundry
Vicki Parry

Permissions
Jan Jensen

And special thanks to the authors of these stories, whose acts of charity and selfless service are an inspiration to us all.

Preface

The scriptures are full of words of wisdom regarding service and charity. The Topical Guide lists over an entire page of citations about service. Prophets and apostles throughout the ages have spoken about the need for heartfelt charity. Jesus instructed us, "Let your light so shine before men, that they may see your good works, and glorify your Father which is in heaven" (Matthew 5:16). And President Spencer W. Kimball said, "The Lord does notice us, and he watches over us. But it is usually through another person that he meets our needs. Therefore, it is vital that we serve each other" (*President Kimball Speaks Out* [Salt Lake City: Deseret Book Co., 1981], 39). Finally, King Benjamin reminds us, "When ye are in the service of your fellow beings ye are only in the service of your God" (Mosiah 2:17).

Clearly charity is a fundamental principle of the gospel. So why is it sometimes hard to serve others? Or to accept service in return? Perhaps because we often think of service in terms of *projects*—something on a grand scale, with long-term benefits, or something that requires multiple people to help. Service couldn't possibly be as simple and spontaneous as delivering a bouquet of wildflowers and a note saying "I'm thinking of you"—could it? And we couldn't possibly be in need of service ourselves, could we?

Service can be that simple. *Good Deeds* is a collection of more than sixty uplifting true stories that celebrate the wonderful spirit that accompanies the acts of kindness and service performed for us and for others. Some stories are from familiar names, but most are from everyday people in everyday situations who have been blessed by someone serving them in everyday ways. Some stories relate experiences where an entire community gathered together to offer help, but most are the quieter acts of service that happen all around us all the time.

Kathleen "Casey" Null enjoys a moment of peace when an impromptu moment of kindness happens at exactly the right time.

Mary Ellen Edmunds is thrilled when a secret someone blesses her life anonymously.

Laurel Christensen shares an experience where the Lord answers her prayer using an unlikely person.

Mark Ellison discovers how a small act of service can change our feelings about those we live and work with.

Sylvia Probst Young finds that her hope is renewed when a friend offers the simplest of services—a listening ear.

Jane Bunker Newcomb learns the power of a smile in brightening up the darkest day.

Ardeth G. Kapp shares a story of a child who undertook an act of service for a neighbor in need.

Richard Siddoway remembers a special Christmas when his small act of service was returned tenfold.

We hope that the stories in this book will inspire and motivate you to count the blessings of the little acts of service that are done to you. And perhaps you will then desire to renew your own efforts to reach out to others in need, more fully activating in your own life the power of doing good deeds.

"You're Going to L.A."

RANDAL A. WRIGHT

Years ago I taught early-morning seminary in southeast Texas. It was not easy having a full-time job, serving on the stake high council, and teaching five mornings a week starting at 5:55 A.M. There were several mornings when I was not as well prepared as I should have been. There were times when I was afraid to stand in front of the class. But those seminary students accepted me as I was and became my friends.

On one occasion, I mentioned that my cousin Ned was getting married in the Los Angeles Temple. Knowing that Ned had been my good friend growing up, someone asked if I was going to his wedding. I replied that I would love to go, but I had to give a talk and sing that weekend and I couldn't afford it anyway. Several weeks later, I walked into the classroom and the students wanted me to play a game. I went throughout the building looking for clues they'd hidden. Back in our classroom, I was instructed to pull the curtains back and read what was written on the chalkboard. I didn't fully grasp the meaning of the message at first. It said:

Put on your rags,
    And shine your shoes.
Grab your bags.
    We've got good news.
We canceled your talk
    And also your song.
You're going to L.A.—
    But not for too long.
You need to go home
    So you can get ready,
For later this evening
    You will see Neddie!
We love you!
    The Seniors of '85

Taped to the board was an envelope that the students encouraged me to open. Inside I found two plane tickets to Los Angeles. These students had saved their money (including lunch money) to buy me a ticket to attend my cousin's wedding. I will never forget the love they showed. They overlooked the days I had come to class unprepared; they loved me and sacrificed for me despite my faults. They truly followed the Savior's admonition, "This is my commandment, That ye love one another, as I have loved you" (John 15:12).

Bakery Store Breakdown

MARY ELLEN EDMUNDS

i want God to be able to use me as an instrument. I want Him to be able to count on me to do what I can to help.

One evening I left work a little bit late. As I was going down Ninth East I saw Matt, one of the fellows I work with, evidently waiting for the bus. So I pulled over, rolled down the window, and said, "Hey, sailor, can I give you a ride?" He laughed but hesitated, saying he lived quite a distance away. I said, "It's right on my way!" He said he knew it wasn't, but I insisted that I could go anywhere I wanted, and if it was on my way, it was on my way. So he got in, and off we went toward his home.

He lived in an apartment right across from a discount bakery place, which he pointed out. As I dropped him off I said I'd go over there and check it out. It was getting close to closing time, and there were only two or three cars in the parking lot. I parked a couple of spots away from one of them and glanced at it as I went in the store. Someone was just sitting in it—probably waiting for someone who'd gone in to do some shopping. I went into the store and wandered around looking at all the good stuff. I got a few loaves of bread, and when I came out I noticed that the car was still in the parking lot. A young woman and two children were sitting inside; I could tell they were having some trouble.

I decided to stop and see if I could help, but I would put my bread in my car first. As I walked past the car with the woman and the children, I was touched with a very strong feeling of compassion. I heard myself say something, but it was as if the words were put into my mind: "I will not leave you alone." It was a very strong, tender feeling. I smiled. I had intended to go over and see if I could help, but that feeling and those words let me know that Someone was watching out for that woman and wanted me to try to help.

I walked over to her and asked if she was having trouble. Yes—she couldn't seem to get her car started. I told her I had jumper cables, but I wasn't sure how to use them. I am not a genius with cars. I'm not an anything with cars besides just knowing how to get them started and how to steer. I asked her to try it again, but when she turned the key there wasn't any noise, so it didn't seem like jumper cables would have helped. I asked if I could call someone for her. Her husband was at work and couldn't be reached. She thought of the number of a neighbor, and I called there but got an answering machine.

She was frustrated, and I didn't know what to do, how to help. I said I would go look in the store for someone who looked nice and smart. A man in there with his wife and son was just checking out. I made myself brave and asked, "Do you know anything about cars?" He kind of shrugged and said he knew a little bit. I asked if he could come and look at a car and see if he could help get it started. He looked at his wife, and she said she and the son would wait.

We went outside, and he looked under the hood. I held the hood up; the latch was broken, so I was the hood holder for the next part of the adventure. He fussed around and had the woman try to start the motor a few times. Meanwhile his wife and son got into their car to wait. I asked how far away he lived, and he said "Price," which was quite a way to go. I was worried that he was going to be late starting back to Price, but he kept trying to find solutions to the problem.

A man watching us from the other side of the fence around the store called out, "Do you need some tools?" The Price Man said he thought maybe that would help, so the Fence Man drove his truck and dog around and into the parking lot and got out a bunch of tools. He was an interesting character, with long, thinning, straggly hair, some of which was in a ponytail, and a long beard. And a can of beer. And a very kind heart. He propped up the hood with a ski pole, which took away one of my responsibilities. But I still held it anyway—afraid it would fall and kill them both.

The Fence Man got busy and helped, and they did lots of stuff, including putting a hole in the radiator hose, which they then had to fix. Finally, after about an hour and a half, they had done what they could and asked her to try again. The car almost started . . . but didn't. I suggested she just lock it up, and I would take her home. I gave the Price Man some wipes for his hands. The Fence Man wore gloves. Both were kind, and we thanked them sincerely, and then they left.

The woman during all this time was trying to keep the kids quiet and calm. At some point she came around and stood near me. She looked at me and said, "You're Sister Edmunds, aren't you?" It caught me off guard, because we'd been there for quite a while by that time. I said, "Yes, I am." Then she said, "I heard you speak at the MTC and at Ricks." We talked about her experiences there a little bit. And from that point on I was thinking, "What if I hadn't helped? What if I had left her alone?"

She had probably heard me share great, glorious ideas about helping each other and serving and doing things even if they're inconvenient and blah blah blah. But would I practice, or just preach?

I try so hard *not* to give talks and then not live what I say. I try to "walk my talk," as I've heard some express it. So that got to me. It was a big lesson. That woman knew who I was. She knew when I walked past her into the store, and she knew when I came out and headed for my car—and when I came back to try to help. I had no idea that she knew. And I wasn't able to do much—I couldn't get her car fixed—but I did what I could. I bundled her, her two children, a car seat, and her purchases into my car and took them home, not too many blocks away. I helped her carry things in. She was grateful. I was, too, more than I could adequately tell her or Heavenly Father. "I will not leave you alone."

Donna and Annie
CONNIE SORENSEN

many people consider nursing homes to be sad places. The residents are usually elderly, infirm in mind or body, or otherwise afflicted. They usually leave only when they die. I, however, found it a wonderful environment for kindness and service. I worked as a nurse at a small facility. We had several residents who were alone in the world, with no family or friends to visit them. We did have volunteers who came in and visited these people on a regular basis. One such volunteer taught me so much about charity and Christlike service that I think the story needs to be told.

Donna* was alone, elderly, and in poor health. She was quiet and kept to herself. Annie* asked the resident services coordinator if she could "adopt" Donna. After careful consideration the coordinator answered yes. The employees at the home assumed that this meant she would visit occasionally and maybe bring a small gift at Christmas. We certainly underestimated Annie. She visited every Sunday. She had a set time, and if she was running late, she called. Donna had difficulty eating, so Annie fed her when she visited, and brought easy-to-eat snacks. Because Donna was

*Names have been changed to honor a request for privacy.

a ward of the state, she had an allowance for clothing, which was sufficient for the basics. Annie provided the little luxuries herself. A pretty outfit to wear on special occasions, warmer slippers, a cuddly robe—things like that. She brought nice lotions, hair accessories, and homey touches to decorate Donna's room. As time passed, Annie's family became involved with Donna and loved her like a grandma. Sometimes Annie's daughters came during the week at suppertime to help Donna eat.

Birthdays and holidays were a treat for Donna. They could have been very sad times for her, even though the staff loved her dearly. If she hadn't had these wonderful people to also love her, special times of the year would have only underscored how alone she was.

As Donna's health declined, Annie called each day. Many times she came in to sit and hold Donna's hand after Donna had received a painful treatment for her illness.

Donna continued to weaken. Annie asked to be called if we thought Donna was going to die. One day the call was made. Donna was fading. Annie rearranged her busy life to sit with Donna. She stayed through the difficult hours, praying for the Lord to comfort and ease Donna. She requested a priesthood blessing for Donna, even though Donna was not a member of the Church. This seemed to comfort both of them.

When Donna passed from this life, Annie was there, holding her hand, crying softly. No words can express the sacred beauty of that moment. But that was not the end of Annie's service to Donna. She arranged a funeral and burial, at her own expense. She took care of everything, including a headstone for the grave. Annie doesn't want her name published, because she feels she has received her reward. What is this reward? The friendship and memory of a wonderful woman named Donna, who had been overlooked by almost everyone else in her life.

Every time I hear the word *charity* I think of the great example set for me by a volunteer.

The Traveling Smile

JANE BUNKER NEWCOMB

I sat on a San Francisco bus going home, tired and depressed after one of those days when nothing seemed to go quite right. It was rush hour, and the bus was packed with people—dull-eyed, tired, aching, and short-tempered.

A large, package-laden lady got on the bus. Every seat was taken, so she had to stand in the aisle near me. *War Horse,* I thought as I looked at her drawn and bitter face. That seemed a pretty good description.

Seated across the aisle next to her was a small, plain-looking lady, someone you wouldn't ordinarily notice. She looked up at "War Horse" and her face was lit with a smile. "Could I hold your packages?" she asked. "It's so hard to stand when your arms are full."

The woman glowered in confusion and looked away. But when she looked back, the smile was still there. Her wrinkled brow eased some as she handed over the packages. "They *are* very heavy," she said. "There are two pairs of specially made shoes for my crippled son, and they weigh twenty pounds a pair." She paused, and the next words seemed very hard for her to say: "Thank you." They chatted on, and as they did, she smiled. Her whole face softened and her body relaxed.

Soon the seated lady got off and the other woman sat down in her place. But her expression had changed, and she smiled up at the young coed standing above her. "Could I hold your books for you? It's difficult to hold on with books sliding every which way."

The girl smiled back, and as she gave up her books I heard her ask, "Did I hear you say you have a son who goes to Jefferson? That's where I go to school."

I had to get off at the next stop, but I imagined that smile traveling all over San Francisco. I too smiled, and wasn't so tired anymore.

An Unlikely Friendship
JEAN DAVIDSON

every garbage-pickup day, four-year-old Colter waits by the front door until the big, rumbling garbage truck screeches to a stop at the front of their house. With a grin as wide as all outdoors, Colter waves until the driver waves back, smiling. On summer days, Colter perches on the front porch steps to wait; on winter days he stands just inside the storm door. The driver never disappoints his little friend and always waves back with a smile.

When Colter fell and broke his arm, the driver noticed the new green cast and hurriedly climbed from the truck to come close and give somber, serious attention to the cast before cheerfully offering to add his autograph alongside all of the other names. Colter was ecstatic!

The friendship continued for more than two years. Then, one bright summer morning, the driver climbed down out of the truck and came around to talk to Colter and his mom. He had a surprise. He had obtained permission from the city to let the little boy climb into the truck for a few minutes to look around and watch as the driver worked the jaws and controls that lifted and emptied the dumpsters into the truck's compactor. Colter had never been happier! He laughed, he giggled, he grinned, he hugged his mom, then he grabbed the hand of the handsome young man and was soon lifted up into the cab of the truck to enjoy a few minutes of time investigating and experiencing the fascinating big machine. The driver, a young father himself, had taken time out to make a little boy's dream come true.

Colter started school a few weeks later, and the driver was promoted to a desk job and gave up his route. Still, for a brief moment in time, two unlikely friends were forever bound by a simple act of kindness. And it all started with a wave, then a smile.

Those Who Mix the Mortar

ARDETH G. KAPP

Some years ago my husband, Heber, and I arose early to go to the laying of the cornerstone for the Jordan River Temple. We planned to arrive well before the crowd, but our plan was ill timed. The crowd was already there when we arrived. Due to the contour of the land, I was stretching to see over the heads of those in front of me. We were on the low side of the slope in front of the temple, and I couldn't see what was going on. Heber, being considerably taller, tried to ease my disappointment by reporting to me observations from his vantage point. "The choir is assembling," he reported. "The General Authorities are taking their places. The TV cameras are in place." This only added to my frustration as I faced the backs of those who were seeing this historic event that I was missing.

After reaching and stretching without success, I decided to settle down, hoping to just feel the spirit of the occasion. It was when I relaxed that my perspective changed and I noticed an activity at the far northeast side of the temple. There I observed two men dressed in dark pants, white shirts, and ties, each holding a shovel. I saw them empty sacks of concrete into a wheelbarrow, pour in water, and mix the contents.

In time, after the choir sang and the presiding authorities had delivered impressive messages, Heber reported that the cameras were moving to the location for the placement of the cornerstone. At that moment the men who had been mixing the mortar pushed the wheelbarrow forward and quickly disappeared behind the scene. Then the cornerstone was anchored in place.

On the television news that evening, I saw what the cameras saw. But they did not see what I had seen. And even today, years later, I never drive past the Jordan River Temple without thinking of those men who mixed the mortar—those whose quiet, unsung labors played a major role in the placement of the cornerstone for the house of the Lord in a building that will stand against all of the storms of life.

Given a choice, would you be willing to serve with the men who mix the mortar? Small acts of service, small sacrifices, small notes and calls, words of encouragement one to another—these "small things" are the mortar that helps hold life together.

"Let's Put a Dollar in Each Shoe"

OSCAR A. KIRKHAM

two boys, playing along a ditch bank, found a pair of shoes at the top of a field. One boy said, "Let's fill them with rocks and see what the owner does."

The other boy said, "Let's put a dollar in each shoe and see what happens."

They followed his suggestion.

The man was watering the field and finally came back to get his shoes, which he had put aside so carefully in order to save them.

When he put his foot into his shoe, he pulled it out again quickly and found the dollar. Then he looked in the other shoe and found another dollar.

Tears came into his eyes, and he knelt on the ground and thanked his Heavenly Father, in a voice filled with emotion, that now he could buy some food to take home to his hungry family. The two boys also went home thankful and happy.

Noah's Christmas Project

LILLIAN WOODLAND

noah Germaine was in a quandary. He had some serious convincing to do. At thirteen years of age he couldn't let his young years overshadow his determination.

Christmas was approaching. Grandpa Max Germaine had worked for many years as a volunteer with the Navajo Indians on the reservation 195 miles north of his home in Mesa, Arizona. Noah had overheard Grandpa say that the kids in one of the Church branches there might not have a Christmas party or receive any gifts.

"Grandpa, I can be responsible for the Christmas party," Noah said. "There isn't much time left, but I know I can do it."

Grandpa replied, "You don't realize how difficult this job could be. There are over a hundred kids in the Indian Wells Branch. If gifts are given, somehow you must obtain a suitable one for each. Where would you get the money? You wouldn't have an organization behind you. Who would help you?"

"I know I can do this. I'll gather support, and believe me, Grandpa, I won't let you down," Noah said.

Fired with enthusiasm, Noah launched his hastily conceived plan. Soon many neighbors, service groups, and local merchants had been informed.

Recruitment didn't intimidate Noah. For instance, he strode into a local supermarket and approached the manager. "Would you help?" he began. "Today I need candy and nuts for more than a hundred kids."

The manager replied, "Are you putting me on?"

Noah said, "No sir, this is for real."

"What is your telephone number?" the manager asked as he disappeared into his office. When he returned he said, "Your mother tells me you are trying to put this Christmas experience together. So, Noah, since she agrees that all this is 'for real,' let's go select the candy you need."

Toys, sports items, books, grooming articles—gifts of all possible varieties—began to accumulate in the Germaine home. Noah's mom and dad and his sisters and younger brother were all involved. Noah organized a gift wrapping party the night before his trip to the reservation. Friends responded with eagerness. Although the atmosphere was lively, they worked steadily, wrapping until eleven o'clock that night.

When Noah surveyed the scene, he tried not to show his dismay. Many of the gifts were still unwrapped. Noah and Grandpa Germaine were to leave at five o'clock in the morning for the difficult winter trip up the mountains to the reservation.

Caught in an emergency, Noah turned to his other grandparents, Grandma and Grandpa Hanna. They arrived minutes later and joined with the family in another nonstop wrapping session.

"Done. We're finally done, Noah," his mother sighed.

Noah was counting. "Not quite," came his labored reply. "We're three boys' packages short."

Noah left the room and quickly returned with his prized marble collection. He filled the kitchen sink with sudsy water, washed, rinsed, dried and polished each marble. He then divided them into two containers, ready for wrapping.

One gift short. What could he do? Without a word, he began unbuckling the strap of the sports watch which encircled his wrist.

"Noah, are you sure?" he was asked.

"Sure? Yes. There will be another time for another watch. Today we're giving a Christmas party," Noah said. And he carefully wrapped the final package.

After Noah returned from the reservation, he was asked, "Well, how did it go?"

Noah answered, "It wasn't easy at first. We were strangers. Our language and customs are different. I think, because we all wanted to be friends, we reached out more than usual. Before long we were sharing, teasing, and laughing. They were very pleased with the gifts we brought. They gave me a gift, too—pottery bowls, a living part of themselves, a part of their heritage."

When asked if it was worth it, Noah answers, "It was the best Christmas I ever had! As I listened to them sing some of my favorite hymns in their native language, I realized that they love the same Father in Heaven I love; they know about the same Joseph Smith I know about. We really are brothers and sisters."

The Lord Chose Jack

LAUREL CHRISTENSEN

my sophomore year at college was a particularly challenging *and* expensive semester. There should be a posting before signing up for certain classes— "Warning: This class requires multiple textbooks you can't afford and will never use." I had to buy the books anyway. I lugged the books home, all the while worrying about my dwindling finances.

That evening, after looking over my checkbook and my student budget, I came to the realization that I could either buy food and gas or pay my tithing. I was exactly $40 short that month. Forty dollars was the difference between keeping a commandment I had never before questioned and being able to eat another month's worth of ramen noodles.

I knelt in prayer that night and asked the Lord for some guidance. I reminded him that I had *always* paid my tithing and asked if there was any way I could just postpone this month's tithing in exchange for life's necessities. I told him I was "good for it" and I just needed a little bit of a break. I asked him to let me know if that was okay. I didn't hear a voice after saying "amen," I just remember walking over to my desk and writing out a check. I knew there wasn't a choice in the matter. The tithing needed to be paid. I remembered the stories in Sunday School and decided that if the Lord can provide an entire family with a mortgage payment or a month's supply of food after they paid tithes and offerings, *surely* he could come up with $40 somewhere for me.

It wasn't ten minutes before the phone rang.

"Hi, it's Jack."

Jack? How could it be Jack? Jack broke my heart and didn't even know it. Jack was the current bane of my college existence. I hadn't spoken to him in weeks—ever since I realized that he wasn't remotely interested in me. Why was *Jack* calling?

I very confidently said, "Oh, yeah, Jack. So, how are you?"

Please be calling to ask me out. Please be calling to ask me out.

"Good. Hey . . . you're going to think this is crazy but I was just writing out a check for my tithing and I had this thought that you probably have always paid your tithing."

My tithing? He had the impression that I pay my tithing? No impression that I'd make a great girlfriend? No thought that the heavens were bringing us together for a reason? Tithing? This didn't look good and I feared I knew where the conversation was going.

"Anyway, I worked some overtime this month and I have some extra money and I don't know why . . . but I just felt like I should call and see if there was anything you needed."

Here was the answer to my prayer.

"Hmmm . . . I'm not sure why you would feel like you should call me. I'm fine. Everything's fine."

I remember thinking, "What are you doing? You're saying *no* to an answered prayer *and* you're lying?"

"Are you sure? Because I sure felt like I should call you."

"Positive. That's so sweet but I don't need a thing."

The phone call ended awkwardly. And suffice it to say I didn't say my prayers again that night. Or the next morning.

About 4:00 the next afternoon there was a knock at the door. I opened it and saw Jack running from my third-floor stairwell. I called his name. He kept running. As I was about to close the door, I saw the envelope with my name on it lying on the welcome mat.

I knew before I opened it what I'd find inside, but I never expected it to be so accurate. Two fresh twenty-dollar bills. Forty dollars. Exactly what I told the Lord I needed. And while he could have inspired my bishop or my parents or a visiting teacher to help me out, he chose to use a source that wasn't so easy to accept.

I've told my tithing story a dozen times and people always say, "No way! Forty dollars? He gave you the forty dollars you needed?" But the lesson I learned was more than "the Lord answers prayers" or "there are blessings for paying tithing." I learned that the Lord uses whomever we need him to use to learn whatever lesson he needs to teach us. The miracle for me was that, of all the people the Lord could have chosen for this good deed, the Lord chose Jack.

The Window-washing Missionary
LINDA AND RICHARD EYRE

Serving with us in England was a sister missionary who believed that proselyting was essentially a process of loving. For her, missionary work was not an all-or-nothing proposition in which you either gave someone the whole gospel and baptized him or gave him nothing at all. Her attitude was to give whatever a person could accept.

She and her companion knocked one day on the door of an older woman who lived alone. "No," she said, she had no interest whatever in hearing their message and began to close the door.

"Then might we help you in *any* way?" said the sister, and her tone of voice left no question that she wanted to do just that.

The older woman hesitated and then asked timidly, "Would you wash a window for me? It is the high one in the entry hall and I can't reach it. I'm afraid if I get up on a chair I might fall. It's the only dirty thing in my house."

The sister washed her window, gladly—with enjoyment.

A month or so later, she was again in the neighborhood and stopped by again to wash the window. She went back every few weeks, asking each time if she could teach the woman of the purpose of life or the restoration or the Book of Mormon. Always the answer was no.

Some time after returning home, the sister received a letter. The writer introduced himself as "a son of the woman whose window you washed." He then said that he and his wife, as well as his sister and her husband, all living in America, had joined the Church. They had contacted the missionaries because of letters from their mother in England who had told them of a sister who had "taught her more of Christ than anyone she had ever met."

The Mean Man Next Door

ANGIE OLSON

i am a mom with three children who at times can be a handful. Elizabeth, my youngest, is seven years old and may very well be the most mischievous child you'll ever meet. She's conniving and fun all at once. She's the one who frustrates us the most but who also keeps laughter in our home. She recently taught me about serving others through kindness.

As I got home Friday evening, April 30, I was greeted at the door by Elizabeth, who shared with me some May Day hanging art she had created in school. As I reached to take it from her and hang it in the living room, she looked at me and said with conviction, "I'm going to give this to the man next door!" A little hurt by her desire to share with him and not me, I questioned her to make sure the man she was talking about was the man I was thinking about.

The neighborhood kids named our neighbor to the east the "mean man." He spends a lot of time and money on his yard, and it is absolutely beautiful. If any child is caught in his yard, he threatens to call the police. He doesn't say anything to anyone and, from what I've seen, doesn't smile. I verified with her that this indeed was the man she was speaking of. I thought to myself, *Let's see if she follows through on this one.*

The next morning was both May Day and Elizabeth's birthday. I really thought that with so much excitement and lots of things to do, she'd forget about her plan. But as we headed out to take her brother to Scouts, she got into the car with the hymnbook (a hard surface to write on) and a plain piece of white paper for the note. We got very busy, and she was happy and thoughtful toward everyone all day.

After lunch she announced to me that she had done it. "I left it for him on his porch!" she said. "I didn't want to bother him, so I didn't even knock on the door. I wonder if he's found it and if he likes it."

The next morning I asked her about the note she'd delivered with her gift. Although somewhat reluctant to share it with me, she told me that the note simply said, "I love you, Your neighbor." I have ever been grateful for her example to me. We now know almost all our neighbors, and we have discovered that the "mean man" next door isn't so mean after all.

"Something I Felt I Should Do"

RACHELLE H. JEPPSON

The car suddenly began to shake violently and a frightening roar filled the interior of the car. I watched anxiously as my grandmother attempted to steer our out-of-control vehicle to safety at the side of the road. Once we had stopped, she got out to examine the car and returned to tell me grimly that we had a badly blown rear tire. Although we were safe, we knew there was no way a young girl and her elderly grandmother would be able to repair the stranded car.

We had started out that afternoon with simple intentions—shopping and running errands. Now we sat nervously contemplating our options, all of which involved crossing the congested multilane freeway. Without access to a telephone and not willing to risk the dash across traffic, I realized that we would have to wait for the assistance of others.

I noticed that a small vehicle had pulled into the emergency lane just down the freeway. "Grandma, look," I said excitedly. "It looks like someone is coming to help us!" As we watched, the small car backed up, and two men climbed out. Their large and unkempt appearance immediately caused me to draw back in fear. As they approached, I noticed that they were covered from head to toe in grease and dirt. "Oh, Grandma," I whispered, "please don't open the door."

My grandmother unrolled the window and the men greeted her cheerfully. "It looks like you've blown a tire," one of the men said. "It just so happens my friend and I are returning home from an automotive conference. Just let me grab my supplies, and we'll have it fixed in no time."

The men retrieved the needed equipment from their truck and proceeded to remove the damaged tire. As I watched the men work, I was awed by their dedication to the task at hand. The pavement was scorching hot from the effects of the blazing overhead sun, yet one man lay on the ground by our car exposing his bare skin to the road. The traffic whizzed by dangerously close to the men, yet they worked with focus and efficiency. With the spare in place, the two men gathered up their belongings and prepared to leave.

"Wait!" My grandmother called out as she reached in the car for her purse. "Please let me reimburse you for your time." The two men politely refused the offer. "At least let me give you money for dinner on the way home," my grandmother insisted. "You've been so kind." The words one of the men spoke next have remained vivid in my memory. Looking my grandmother in the eye, he replied earnestly, "I recently became a member of The Church of Jesus Christ of Latter-day Saints. This is just something I felt I should do." Warmed by the simple beauty of the words that had been spoken, I watched as the men returned to their car.

The service that was rendered on my behalf that sunny afternoon reaches far beyond the simple scope of the act itself. It has enabled me to examine my personal motivations for service and to further appreciate those who have served me throughout the years. Though caution in similar situations is often warranted, I am grateful that the man responded to the prompting that alerted him to our damaged car and that my grandmother agreed to accept his assistance. The motivation behind his act of service was both simple and pure and taught me that meaningful lessons can come from unexpected circumstances and unlikely sources.

Gifts from the Heart

ARDETH G. KAPP

It was Christmas Eve. The magic of Christmas seemed more real that year, not so much because of lights and tinsel, but because we had a feeling of excitement from the inside out. Family members had gathered at our house for our traditional dinner. Then Grandpa gathered us in the living room, opened the Bible, and read once again the Christmas story from Luke.

After the stockings were finally hung and treats left for Santa, the children reluctantly, yet eagerly, went to bed. They tried hard to get to sleep while listening intensely for any sounds from the expected night visitor.

"Now, if Heber would just go to bed, I could finish my gift for him," I said to myself. I had been working on this gift for my husband for about three months, and I needed about three more hours to complete it. But despite my encouragement for him to leave the room, he kept lingering. It was evident he would wait for me. I decided to go to bed and wait until he dropped off to sleep; then I'd slip out and finish his present.

With the lights out and the house quiet, I lay in bed looking into the dark, too excited to sleep. I listened for his heavy breathing, which would let me know it was safe to slip away. To my amazement, after a little while he whispered, "Ardie." I didn't respond. A conversation now would only delay the time when I could finish my project. To my great surprise, when I didn't answer he slipped out of bed as cautiously as I had planned to.

"What is he up to?" I wondered. I couldn't get up then. I waited and waited, but he didn't return. What should I do? Maybe if I went to sleep, I could awaken at about three o'clock and finish my project before everyone got up at about six, the time Grandpa Ted had agreed that we should all gather around the tree.

I was aroused from sleep when Heber got into bed ever so quietly. Only a few minutes later, his heavy breathing assured me he was sound asleep. It was three o'clock.

Months earlier, we had talked about Christmas and made the traditional gift list that ranged from the ridiculous to the sublime. At the top of my list was a wish that we could have more time together so he could teach me his great understanding of the gospel. I was driving two hours each day to BYU, and his schedule was very busy. Our time together was precious.

Heber's list of wants was short, as usual, but he did express a concern for the responsibility he had as a stake president to lead the way for his stake members, and it bothered him that his family history was not compiled. His family group sheets were incomplete.

My gift to him was finally wrapped. I could hardly believe I had done it, but there it was—the evidence of many hours of work. I hurried back and slipped into bed just in time to hear children's voices from the other room. "Grandpa says it's time to get up. Hurry! We can't wait!" they said. Neither could I.

In the living room Heber handed me a package. I opened it and found a box of cassette tapes. On top of the box was a message: "My dear Ardie, While you are traveling each day, I will be with you. As you know, the Doctrine and Covenants has been of special interest to me over the years. I have enjoyed reading and recording for you the entire book. Reading it with the purpose of sharing it with you, I have endeavored to express my interpretation and feelings so that you might feel what I feel about this sacred book. I finished it only a few hours ago. May these tapes add to your wisdom and help unfold the mysteries of God and prepare us for our eternal life together."

Then I handed Heber my gift. He tore off the wrapping, and inside was a book of remembrance—many pages of pictures and stories never before recorded, a result of secret trips to visit and interview relatives and the assembling of records and histories.

On the first page of the gift was a message: "Dear Heber, As I have copied, reviewed, and prepared these sheets and interviewed family members, your ancestors have become very real to me, and I have an increased appreciation and understanding of the greatness and nobility in the man I married. Although I never met your father, and met your mother only once, when I meet them I know I'll love them and know them better because of this gift I have prepared for you, which really has been a gift for me."

I don't remember any of the other gifts we received that year, but Heber and I will never forget the spirit of that glorious Christmas celebration.

"Not So Different from Me"

PATRICIA T. HOLLAND

most of us are well acquainted with the responsibilities of service. I am sure many of you have baked cookies until your spatulas melted or baby-sat your neighbor's children until your brains sputtered. Occasionally when I am in such situations I fear my fatigue will slip into resentment, and then I wonder if being stretched so thin may not only prevent my developing new charity but actually diminish the supply I thought I had. I have learned, however, that though we may not have a completely willing heart every time we serve, such service molds our heart, blesses us, and does enlarge our capacity to give. We must remember, too, during periods of our lives in which we feel that all we can do is keep our own immediate circle of families or friends afloat, that *emotional* and *spiritual* service to others can sometimes be as important as physical acts.

My daughter, Mary, tells of being assigned as a visiting teacher to a friend but procrastinating the visit because her friend, who had three preschoolers and was pregnant with a fourth child, always seemed frazzled and frustrated. Mary knew she would want to shoulder some of her friend's tasks, but she also felt stretched to the limit with two preschoolers of her own, a husband in graduate school, and a demanding Church calling.

The idea of having three more children in her two-room apartment adding to her own children's chaos, even for only a few hours, seemed overwhelming. Yet, partially out of duty, but mostly out of love and a desire to lift her friend's spirits, she regularly offered to tend, clean house, and relieve her of some of her other burdens. Occasionally those offers were accepted; more often they were declined. Even when her friend accepted help, Mary could see little difference in her friend's mood.

One day, when Mary herself was having a particularly exasperating day, she called her friend—in the spirit of good visiting teaching—just to tell her that she couldn't help thinking of her and empathizing with her struggles. During that conversation, Mary sensed a gradual change in that sister's attitude, a kind of happiness she hadn't sensed in her very often.

Near the end of the conversation, her friend admitted to feeling nearly ecstatic to realize that Mary, who seemed to be able to handle everything with grace and goodwill, was having a miserable day. The sister explained, "Mary, I am so grateful. I've never had anyone share their frustrations with me. They are always terribly concerned about mine, and they just know I can't handle any others. Your honesty has made me feel so much better. I didn't think you ever felt frazzled like I do. I have always thought you were perfect. But today I see that you are not so different from me. Maybe I am doing just fine. I don't really need help as much as I just need to know that I am normal. Thanks!" Offering someone our companionship and our honest shared sorrows as well as joys is as important as performing a physical task for them.

A Child's Kiss

CAROL GEIL

On the wall of our child care center in Creede, Colorado, there is a copy of the writing "Children Learn What They Live" by Dorothy Law Nolte. I recently witnessed a lovely example of what this poem means.

Creede Child Care Center is a small center serving a mixed age group ranging from one-year-old toddlers to school-aged children. One of our mothers, in saying good-bye to her four-year-old son, lightly kissed him on the top of his head and then gently said good-bye to the other children around the table with him. Later, when we were playing a circle game, the young boy moved next to a one-year-old girl, who had been a little fussy, and began to comfort her. Just then, he was chosen to be "it" in our game. As he got up to play the game, he gently kissed the toddler on the top of her head.

When children live with caring and affection, they learn to show it to others.

"My Choice Is You!"
MARK BYBEE

Kirk knocked on the door of the room where I was teaching a seminary class and asked if he could come in and ask a girl to one of the main dances at the school. Kirk was a state champion wrestler, a football player, and a handsome, popular athlete with whom any girl would love to have a date.

As Kirk wandered around the room—back and forth, up and down the aisle, with roses in his hand—he recited a poem of love and caring and a desire to take a particular girl to the dance. Every girl watched with anticipation as he strolled towards her, and then with a forlorn expression as he passed her by.

The most bright-eyed girl in the room was Becky, not because of anticipation on her own behalf but because of her love for life, her caring for all the other girls in the class, and her excitement for these types of curious activities in the classroom. Anticipation for herself was the furthest thing from her mind—she had been confined to a wheelchair for many years because of a long-term disease. Her eyes glistened and her smile broadened as Kirk continued to pace around the room and recite his poem. The entire class broke into a sigh followed by tears from every eye as Kirk placed the flowers on Becky's desk and proclaimed: "And my choice is you! Will you go with me?"

Becky's emotions would not allow her to answer at that time, so Kirk just asked her to think about it and then left. It is my understanding that the date was a complete success. Kirk took her out on the floor in her wheelchair and danced all around her as she danced within her chair. On the last dance of the evening he picked her up out of the chair and danced all around the dance floor with her cradled in his arms as she laughed and cried. I'll never forget her expression on the last day of class as we had a small testimony meeting. There Becky expressed thanks for that experience and said she could hardly wait for the resurrection, when she would be able to "dance and dance and dance."

Help from the Prophet Joseph

MARGARETTE McINTIRE BURGESS

My older brother and I were going to school, near to the building which was known as Joseph's brick store. It had been raining the previous day, causing the ground to be very muddy, especially along that street. My brother Wallace and I got fast in the mud, and could not get out, and of course, child-like, we began to cry, for we thought we would have to stay there. But looking up, I beheld the loving friend of children, the Prophet Joseph, coming to us. He soon had us on higher and drier ground. Then he stooped down and cleaned the mud from our little, heavy-laden shoes, took his handkerchief from his pocket, and wiped our tear-stained faces. He spoke kind and cheering words to us and sent us on our way to school rejoicing.

Rachel, My Sister

LEAH CHAPPELL,
AS TOLD TO MARILYNNE LINFORD

The bishop called to ask if he could come over tonight," said my husband, Wayne, in his "I know something you don't know" voice.

"Do you know why?" I asked.

"Yes, a new calling for you," he said.

My mind raced from the nursery to the Relief Society, then bounced back to the Primary and through the library, wondering what the new calling would be. Then panic struck as I remembered. Sister Coke had been released as a counselor in our special Relief Society. "Oh, no," I thought.

Within our ward boundaries is a large rest home. The wards in the stake take turns being responsible for the Church services there—including sacrament meeting and Relief Society. The rest home is a dependent branch, and it was our ward's turn to provide the branch presidency and Relief Society presidency.

I had been in the rest home once before on a substitute visiting teaching assignment. That visit had depressed me so much that I had told the Relief Society president I could not go again.

That evening, as I met with the bishop, my fears were realized. "Sister Chappell," he said, "Sister Marlene Recksiek, as president of the rest home Relief Society, has asked for you as her second counselor. Sister Clara Harrison will continue as the first counselor. We feel this is a special calling. Will you accept this call from the Lord?"

The bishop had the nicest way of saying the worst things.

"I'll try," I muttered.

As I met with the other two sisters in the presidency on Thursday for an orientation, I could scarcely believe what I heard.

"Oh, just wait, Leah," said Marlene. "After you've been with us a week or two, you'll love it."

"The sisters are so special," Clara said.

Marlene added, "I was called for one year. But when the year was up, I begged the bishop to let me keep this job longer. It's been almost two years now."

Sunday came. I arrived at the rest home an hour early, as we had planned in our presidency meeting. We had a prayer, and then each of us took a list of sisters we were to help get to the meeting. A few of the women, I learned, were able to come by themselves, but the majority needed help to get from their rooms to the recreation room where sacrament meeting was held. Since this was my first week, Marlene had given me a list of only five sisters to help.

I got the first four to the recreation room with remarkable ease. Each was eager to attend the meeting. Two of them were already in their wheelchairs waiting for me when I arrived. They directed me to the elevators and down the right halls to the recreation room. "I'm being blessed," I thought. "Maybe this won't be so bad after all."

The fifth name on my list was Rachel—room 207. I knocked softly on her door. She immediately opened it. "Oh, good," I thought. "She can walk."

"I've come to take you to church," I said.

"I can't go," Rachel replied. "My sister is coming to visit me."

"Oh, that will be nice," I said. "Well, I'll come for you again next week. I hope you can come then."

During the next few weeks, I watched Rachel. I learned that in the ten years she had been in the rest home she had never had a visit from her family. She had never attended church while she had been in the rest home, though her records said that she was LDS. I learned that she often went outside on the sidewalk to watch for the sister who never came.

Each week I went to Rachel's room to ask her to come. I prayed for her. I felt that we could take away at least a little of her loneliness if she would just come to the meetings.

On the sixth Sunday, I knocked on her door.

"I've come to take you to church," I said.

"I can't," she replied as usual. "My sister is coming to see me."

Then the inspiration I had been praying for came.

"Rachel," I said, "My name is Leah. In the Bible, Leah and Rachel are sisters. I will be your sister."

Confusion filled Rachel's eyes. I repeated, "I am Leah. The Bible says Leah and Rachel are sisters."

After a moment, Rachel looked up at me with a light I had never seen in her eyes before. She put her hand in my outstretched one. As we walked toward the recreation room, I gave her hand a little squeeze. "Sisters," I said.

The Night I Fell in Love
with My Daughter's Boyfriend

LARENE GAUNT

It started out as an rather ordinary night, that night I fell in love with my daughter's boyfriend. My husband and son were away on a trip together and so it was just me and my daughter, Lisa, at home. I was working on some family history in the office and my daughter's boyfriend, Tracy, had come to keep us company. I quite liked Tracy. I had met him a couple of times before and thought he was nice though I wanted to get to know him better.

The kids invited me to watch a movie with them, but I told them to go ahead, I still had some work to do. Tracy popped the video into the VCR as Lisa headed for the bathroom next to my office. Instead of hearing the door swing open, I heard a dull clunk, and then Lisa peeked her head around the corner.

"Mom? Do you know how to fix a doorknob?" In one hand was half of a door-knob, in the other hand was the other half.

"What happened?" I asked.

"I don't know. I just twisted the knob and it kept twisting and then it came off."

"Are you guys ready?" Tracy appeared in the hallway behind Lisa. "The movie's about to start." He saw the broken knob and frowned. "What's up?"

"I guess I don't know my own strength," Lisa grinned.

The bathroom door swung slowly on its hinges. For the last couple of months, I had noticed that the door had a tendency to drift open on its own unless locked shut. I had been meaning to have my husband fix it, but he was gone and it was just us. And none of us knew the first thing about home repair.

"Do you know how to fix a doorknob?" I asked Tracy.

"No, but I'll give it a shot," he said without hesitation. "C'mon, Lisa, let go door-knob shopping."

An hour later, the three of us stood in the hallway outside the bathroom with our tools in hand and a new doorknob still in the package.

"What's first?" Tracy asked, rolling up his sleeves. As Lisa held the door steady for him, I handed him the tools he needed. Tracy worked hard to get that knob attached to the door, and when he was finished we stepped back to admire his handi-work. It was beautiful; it only had one flaw—it didn't work. Tracy had attached the knob on backward so the lock was on the outside of the door rather than on the inside.

"Don't worry," he said. "I can fix it." And he knelt down by the door again. Once more he wrestled with the door and the knob and once more he attached the pieces. And once more it didn't work.

I looked from Lisa to Tracy and back again. "Now what?" I asked.

"Let's try this," Tracy said. "Here, Lisa, help me hold this."

Over the next hour or so I watched as the two of them worked with the door and the knob, trying every way they could think of to fasten it properly. Once it was upside down, once they accidentally used the back half of the old knob with the front half of the new one. It was turning out to be quite a project.

Five times Tracy attached and reattached that doorknob. Five times he had to start over, but each time he just smiled and said, "Don't worry, I can fix it." And he would try again. And when he did finally get the knob to twist the right way with the lock on the inside of the door and all the pieces in the right places, he sat back and said, "Cool. Now I know how to fix a doorknob."

It was just a simple act of service on a random, ordinary evening. Most people probably wouldn't have given it a second thought. But Tracy did more than just fix a doorknob for me. He showed me the qualities of his character. I saw that he was eager to help, he was creative, he was willing to make mistakes and to learn from them. Most impressive to me, though, was that he was persistent; he wanted his work to be *right*, not just *all right*.

And he worked well with my daughter. They laughed and joked through the entire project, anticipating the other's thought or need as if they had been fixing doorknobs together their entire lives. I could see that they had a special connection and the thought of the two of them together fit perfectly. Like they were two halves of a perfectly fitted doorknob.

Statistics of Service

LAURIE HANSEN

The following is a letter to the editor I wrote expressing my deep gratitude for the many heroes who helped my family during a time of great trial.

My husband was diagnosed with colon cancer eighteen months ago and died this month at the age of forty-four. I was unable to keep track of visits, phone calls, and many expressions of love. But I did write down many of the acts of kindness we received. One small act of kindness, which may seem insignificant or trivial by itself, when combined with many other such acts can mount up to immense support.

During the last eighteen months we received over 100 meals, 125 plates of bakery goods, and over 500 cards or letters of good wishes. Approximately 270 people have donated money, 70 have given gifts, over 300 people have contributed toward flowers. I kept track of at least 375 acts of time or labor. The people I work with donated over 130 hours of their own vacation time so that I could have more time with Greg, giving us the greatest gift they could: time together while he was alive. People we didn't even know gave us a condominium in Hawaii for a week, and others gave us the money to finance the trip. A stay at a beach house, tickets to Disneyland, and airline tickets for our entire family, along with spending money to enjoy two full weeks in southern California were given last year so that our five daughters could enjoy their father while he still felt well. Use of a home in St. George was provided for several quick getaways. At the time Greg was diagnosed we were in the middle of building an addition on our home. Many came to help him complete the task he had started.

At times when I felt discouraged, someone would call, drop off a treat, or send just the right card. Baptists, Catholics, Episcopalians, Jews, Lutherans, Methodists, Mormons, Presbyterians, and many others offered prayers in our behalf. I figure that if every person who sent a card, meal, or treat also prayed once a day for us over the last eighteen months, it would amount to 396,575 prayers! In truth, I know there were more than five times that amount, for entire families, congregations, and prayer groups also prayed for us, many of them more than once a day.

I'd like to thank everyone from the bottom of my heart. You have pulled me through hard times and instilled in me a love for mankind for which I will be forever grateful.

"I Think You Have a Fire at Your Store"

LaRUE H. SOELBERG

This Christmas had begun like any other. The laughter of our happily excited children was evidence that Santa had indeed been able to decipher the hastily scrawled notes mailed weeks before.

As was our custom, LeRoy and I would wait until the children had sufficient time to inspect, test, compare, and segregate their new treasures before we would open our gifts.

The similarity of this Christmas to any other ended here.

The loud knock on the front door demanded immediate answer.

"Come quick!" There was urgency in our friend's voice. "I think you have a fire at your store!"

Fears flooded my mind as I ran through the vacant lot to the store, a small grocery business, which was not yet half paid for.

There were no flames rising from the building, but the windows were solid black.

A fireman came running up and put his hand against the window.

"No heat." He seemed relieved. "There's no fire now—let's open it up."

Our hopes were raised. Perhaps we had not lost everything!

He turned the key and pushed open the door. The dense choking smoke that had filled every minute space of the small building drifted out into the street.

My heart sank. It was like looking at the inside of a coal-black furnace. Not a crack, not a corner, not one can stacked beneath another had escaped the ugly black filth!

LeRoy, with the help of some of the firemen, removed the refrigerator-case motor that had burned itself out. We stood gazing in disbelief at the result.

True, the store had not burned, but was it salvageable? Perhaps the building and equipment could be cleaned, but what about the thousands of bottles, cans, and cartons? Even if they could be saved, how could we possibly survive the closing of business for even a few days?

"Only one thing to do." The fireman's voice was surprisingly cheerful. "Let's see if we can clean it up."

We were reluctant to accept his offer of help. After all, wasn't this Christmas, a day to be spent with family and loved ones?

"Come on," he joked. "My son will be glad to have me out of the house so that he can play with his electric train. Get me a bucket and some soap."

No sooner would we equip one volunteer with cleaning items than another would appear at the door, demanding, as one neighbor put it, "a chance to participate in this joyful holiday project."

Each person who came to the door uttered an astonished "Oh no!" and then, "Where do you want me to start?"

By 11 A.M. there were more than forty people: friends, neighbors, firemen, patrons, and new acquaintances scrubbing away at the terrible black goo. Still they kept coming! We were overwhelmed.

The men had taken over the cleaning of the ceiling, the most stubborn and difficult task of all. The women were working in twos, taking items off the shelves, cleaning what they could and boxing the rest.

One young lad who was recuperating from a broken leg made trips to the cafe to get hamburgers and potato chips to feed the workers. Another brought turkey and rolls which, I'm certain, were to have been the biggest part of the family's Christmas dinner.

An energetic teenager must have run twenty miles altogether emptying buckets and refilling them with clean hot water.

A service station operator brought hundreds of old cleaning rags.

An electrician worked on a motor replacement and soon had the refrigerator case operating again.

This was no ordinary cleaning job. Every inch had to be scrubbed, scoured, washed, and rinsed. Sometimes this procedure had to be repeated seven times before the white of the walls and ceiling would show through, yet everyone was laughing and joking as though they were having a good time.

"Actually, I only dropped by to supervise," came a comment from behind the bread rack.

"I bet this cures you of following fire trucks," a fireman chided his wife.

We all laughed when an attractive blond woman, who was perched on top of the vegetable case and now bore a striking resemblance to a chimney sweep, burst out with a chorus of "Chim Chim Cheree."

It was shortly after 2 A.M. when we locked the front door. Everyone had gone. As they finished their jobs, they just slipped out—not waiting for a word of thanks or a smile of appreciation.

We walked home hand in hand. Tears flowed freely down my cheeks. Not the tears of frustration and despair that had threatened earlier, but tears of love and gratitude. Business would open as usual tomorrow—because fifty-four kind people had the true spirit of Christmas in their hearts.

Our children had left the tree lights burning, and our presents lay unopened in a neat pile on the floor. They would wait until morning. Whatever those gaily wrapped packages contained would be dwarfed, indeed, by the great gift of friendship given to us that Christmas Day.

The Great "Bale-Out"

EDGAR E. EATON

grant Tracy grumbled as he wrestled with his hay crop just outside of Carbonado, Washington. A rainstorm threatened. This was July, when it's not supposed to rain, even in usually damp Puget Sound country. But the clouds wrapped themselves around each other like huge clumps of dirty cotton, dark and rumbling. And a thunderstorm would ruin his hay.

To top it off, Brother Tracy had promised his barn to the stake youth that night for a barn dance following their annual youth conference. Even with the help of his sons and their families, Brother Tracy was convinced he would never get the hay in before the rain, and the teenagers on their way only accentuated his problem.

For six hours that morning the 200 Auburn Washington Stake teenagers and 50 leaders had cleaned yards and homes, painted inside and out, put booklets together, fixed food, cleaned headstones in a cemetery, and helped with children.

For six hours they had fun together helping others. Then they cleaned up and returned to church for dinner and a testimony meeting. Now it was fun and games time at the Tracys'. They arrived in cars, vans, and pickups—ready to dance. And dance they did until around 10:00 P.M. It was about then that Chris and Jeff Williams of the Buckley Ward, who had worked for Brother Tracy on the farm at times, could see that even though he had finished baling the hay, he was going to have trouble getting it in the barn before the storm.

Chris and Jeff went to Rae Dell Killstrom, one of the Young Women leaders, and told her they were going to "buck hay." A self-declared "city slicker," Sister Killstrom thought that they meant they were going to go play in the hay. Picturing them with hay all over them she said no, if they left the dance they couldn't come back.

But then Sister Killstrom talked with Geraldine Tracy, Grant's wife. Once she understood the problem, she talked with other stake leaders and found that some of them had just been discussing the same thing. And that was it. As soon as the problem was explained to the kids, there was no hesitating. With no gloves and with bare arms, they marched out, swarming over the fields like seagulls attacking crickets.

By then it was pitch dark and lightning danced across the sky, illuminating groups of young people everywhere, racing the weather. Within an hour the hay was in the barn and stacked—stacked by a bunch of kids in their party clothes.

Grant Tracy was overwhelmed. "Oh, man, I'll tell you, it was unbelievable," he recalls. "It just gave me . . ." He breaks off, searching for the right words. "You could see kids all over the field." He pauses again. "It would bring tears to anyone's eyes. It couldn't have been a more perfect ending to their conference."

If Grant Tracy ever builds a monument on his farm, it won't have a seagull on it. It'll be a golden replica of a teenager with a smile on his face and a bale of hay in his hands.

Special Delivery

SHANE DIXON

dad has a blue jacket that is a size too big for him. He wears a hat he calls lucky and Mom calls old. He has shirts that I grew up with—literally—and that show less signs of aging than I do. He has a motorcycle with a muffler we can hear from a half mile away, allowing us to set the dining room table before he ever walks into the door. And as his three sons we also were proud to practice frugality.

I started my career as a paperboy at the age of twelve, along with my brother, who was thirteen. I paid ten percent of my earnings for tithing, gave twenty percent to my father for my mission, and the rest I could spend on my personal affairs (which often involved various attempts to single-handedly consume a dozen donuts). I learned the value of work young, and eventually I saved enough to purchase a bike.

For six years I rode a bike around local neighborhoods delivering papers. Old ladies would request them on the porch, young couples asked for them in the mailbox, and some would complain when I let the rubber band snap, causing advertisements to slide smoothly across the driveway (I was frugal, not efficient). My lack of efficiency was caused at least in part by a heavy workload of school, athletics, and church activity. I suppose part of frugality involves not only stretching a dollar but stretching time as well. My older brother and I both woke up as early as 4:30 in the morning to deliver papers that covered a twelve-mile radius.

My father was also consumed with a workload as a teacher and a bishop. He often spent long hours in dedicated labor to help those outside the family that needed him. We seemed to understand this, but also realized that this often cut into the time he could have otherwise spent with us.

As Christmas approached one year I looked with fear to the holiday edition of the newspaper, notorious for its size. The Christmas edition had that uncanny ability of being so large that it could topple the weak-armed boy who attempted to throw it without placing his feet sturdily on the ground.

On Christmas Eve I had figured out that I'd have to wake up at 4:00 in the morning in order to finish the route by the 7:30 deadline. The clouds outside had all the signs of rain, and I dreaded the idea of having the cold weather freeze my hands as my fingertips strained to hold onto the plastic-bagged two-by-fours. My brother and I set our clocks for the awful hour and went to sleep. I slept with the uneasy picture that Christmas excitement didn't begin with awaking from peaceful slumber.

What happened was infinitely worse. I awoke to the flash of my alarm clock reading 12:00 A.M., a sign that power had stopped during the night. I ran downstairs to check another clock. It was ominous and unbending: 7:30 A.M. I ran back upstairs in a state of panic and into my brother's room. "The alarm. 7:30. Christmas." I ran back downstairs, leaving my brother with no help at deciphering my cryptic babbles.

Past the Christmas tree in the living room and out the front door, I flew into the driveway to discover the papers were not in their appropriate place. What was the delivery truck *doing?* It was *Christmas!* I calmed myself from complete panic by telling myself it was raining. Perhaps the papers had been moved inside.

I moved back toward the house and noticed I had forgotten my shoes. The socks on the slick pavement caused me to slip my way back into the house. My brother had made his way downstairs and we looked at each other. I asked if the papers were in the garage. He said no. We came to a silent conclusion and then we both spoke.

"Dad," we said.

The reality of what had occurred came to me some time later. My father had gotten up in the early morning to do two paper routes for his sons. He had sabotaged our alarm clocks, stolen copies of our route lists, and had thrown some 120 papers out the window of an old VW bus. The rain must have come inside the car, because the next time I saw him he was as wet as my socks.

I met him on his way to the house, and he stopped in his tracks when he saw me. He stood on the driveway in his large, wet jacket. He looked at me for a second, and I was filled with a feeling of thankfulness as I realized I had been given the gift of a few hours of holiday freedom.

I'm not sure what touched me so much about this gift from my father. I guess it was the fact that he was willing to be as worn out as his clothes. He was willing to be stretched out and worn thin—all for a few hours of added happiness for his family. This was evident in the words he spoke to me on the driveway. His words were simple.

"I was hoping to finish before you got up."

I walked back into the house hugging my dad in his oversized jacket, content in my rain-slicked socks.

"This Is All the Money I Have"

ARDETH G. KAPP

The kindly old man didn't go outside as much anymore, and he didn't cross the street over to the Gardners' home as he used to. During the winter he had been there many times, not only to the Gardners' home but also to the homes of neighbors up and down both sides of the street. After a heavy snowstorm he was usually out at the crack of dawn to clear the snow from driveways, providing a happy surprise in the early morning hours for grateful neighbors and friends. In the summertime he carefully arranged selected vegetables in baskets and carried them across the street to share with his neighbors. But it was not his vegetables that made him so popular with the children so much as the sweets he always had for them when they came around to the back door. His dear wife, restricted to a wheelchair, insisted on including "something sweet for the children" in their weekly shopping list.

Another winter season was slipping away, yielding to the warm sun of springtime. With this season came other signs of ebbing away. The old gentleman's garden had been planted with much difficulty this year. He tended it less often than usual, but enough, he hoped, to assure a good harvest that he might share one last time with his neighbors and friends. His good health was gone. His service to his friends was now greatly restricted. Some days were difficult and some were long for both him and his wife. "The very worst thing about being sick," he explained, "isn't the pain so much as the feeling of being so useless." He swallowed hard to keep the tears under control and forced a smile into the careworn lines on his face.

Across the street in the home of the Gardners, young Elizabeth, only seven and a half years old, had acquired a keen sense of concern for others. In her family, when anyone had a problem or felt unhappy, the family members discovered little ways to cheer each other up. Over her few short years, this child had seen her faithful mother find time to wipe a tear, heal a wound with a kiss, and listen to the never-ending account of a child who needed her attention. It was not just within the busy yet happy setting of her home that Elizabeth witnessed this activity. The same concern was expressed by her mother in many ways beyond her home, up and down the street, as the children distributed hot cinnamon rolls to many, or a dinner for a family on a special occasion.

One day young Elizabeth left her home quietly without telling anyone what was on her mind or in her hand. She looked both ways, then crossed the street. She was not carrying hot cinnamon rolls from her mother's kitchen as she had often done before. She came carrying her own treasures. She walked quietly through the carport overgrown with vines breaking into bud and made her way under the balcony to the back door with the little glass window in it. She rang the bell at the home of the kind old man and his dear wife, then quickly hurried to hide behind the large bush of Oregon grape.

Inside the home the old couple looked at each other and wondered who would be calling at this hour. The man, with some effort, eased himself up from his chair, stretched his back before taking a step, then shuffled toward the door. As he opened the door, his wife strained to hear a voice that she might identify. There were birds in the feeder that he attended to each day, but no one was in sight. He stepped out to look around, looking first one way, then the other, but there was no sign of anyone.

As he turned to come in, he noticed a torn piece of paper on the step by the door. It was a piece of newsprint, the kind he had seen children carry home from school. The paper had writing on it, and on top of the paper were two coins—a nickel and a quarter. Steadying one hand on his leg, he reached to the ground to pick up the note and the money. He could see that a message had been printed by a child.

By now his wife was calling, "Ted, is someone there?" She called again. "Ted?"

He shuffled back into the living room. "No one was there," he said in a quiet voice.

"Then what do you have in your hand?"

"Someone has been here," he said. "Look at this."

He sat beside his wife on the couch, and together, straining to see through their glasses, they read these few words: "Dear Mr. and Mrs. Greene, you are very dear friends of ours, you are always nice to us. Here is something you might need. From Elizabeth Gardner." Words barely hanging on the bottom of the edge of the page completed the message: "This is all the money I have."

Holding the paper in one hand, he opened his other hand to show his wife. There in the palm of a trembling hand lay the nickel and quarter. "All the money she has," he whispered. "A mite." His wife removed her glasses to wipe a tear from her eye and brushed a lock of gray hair from her forehead. "Like a widow's mite," he added.

Together they sat holding the small piece of paper and two coins while they thought of a plan.

Walking with the help of a cane, Brother Greene made his way over to the Gardners' home, knocked on the door, and asked to speak to Elizabeth. She came to the door, her chin buried in her neck while she looked at the floor. The old man stooped over to wrap her in one of his arms while he steadied himself with his cane. Giving her a gentle hug, he thanked her for all she had done to make him and his wife so happy. The child smiled and looked up at her mother, who was now standing at her side, curious to know what her daughter had done. Elizabeth then told her mother about her visit to the Greenes.

"In our family we think of little things to do for people or give to them if they are feeling bad," she said. "We write notes to each other and leave little things like a cookie or a piece of candy. One time one of my sisters carved a little heart out of soap to go with a note she wrote to me when I was feeling unhappy." In a matter-of-fact tone Elizabeth added, "I got the idea from what we do in our family, and I decided to take it outside my family. I could see that Brother and Sister Greene were getting old, and I thought they might need to pay hospital bills or something." Then in a happy tone she concluded, "So I gave them all the money I had."

Now Brother Greene felt not so useless after all. There were still lessons to learn and people to serve. The following Sunday the aged man and the sensitive child visited with the ward clerk. "We'd like to make a contribution," they said, "a contribution of one nickel and one quarter to help build the new temple."

The Day We Picked the Beans

MABEL GABBOTT

that summer was the most prolific bean summer we could remember. Every morning Mama said, "Up early now and see if there are any beans ready for canning." There always were. Day after day, we picked early, and we canned during the morning hours. When the best of the beans were bottled, and the picking grew thinner and thinner, we began to nod conspiratorially at one another. Bean canning was done for another summer.

Then one day Mama looked across the road to the Evans's bean patch.

"I do believe she needs help," she said.

That evening Mama went over to see Marie. They walked through the garden, talking and pinching and nodding. We watched and sighed.

It wasn't that Marie wasn't just as energetic as Mama (she was even younger), and ever so hardworking (she worked downtown each day), or that she needed the canned beans any the less for her family (she had little children). It was just that Mama had a terrific green thumb, a deep respect for any growing thing, and a horror of waste. She couldn't let those beans get one day older or tougher.

The next morning, earlier than usual, there was Mama.

"Up, everyone!" she called cheerily, "We are picking beans today."

"But, Mama," we hesitated. "Ours are all in bottles."

"The Evans's beans are not," said Mama. "Up now, quickly!"

We carried Marie's bottles across the road to our kitchen and scalded them. We picked basket after basket of beans. We sat on our screened back porch and snapped beans.

Mama was in the hot kitchen, canning them as fast as we had some ready. It didn't matter that we thought some were too old. They would be nourishing when summer greens were gone, Mama explained.

When Marie came home, after gathering up her little children, she found her bean patch harvested and bottles and bottles of beans to store against a cold white winter.

We grumbled as we stooped to pick the beans, and we groaned as we swished away summer flies while we snapped the beans; but being young and experienced in sharing such family ventures, we sang songs and shared stories as bean after bean found its way into its winter storage place.

And somehow now when I think of our small town and our screened back porch, of summer gardens and Mama, I think of the day we picked our neighbor's beans. And each time I remember, my mother grows wiser and dearer.

A Simple Prayer

BEATRICE D. BULLEN

my heart was pounding as I awaited my new daughter. "I must be as frightened as she is," I thought. "I wonder if she is scared to be joining our family. What will she be like? Will we be able to show her our love? Will she love us?"

It was seven o'clock in the morning, and my husband and I and five of our children were sitting tensely in the chapel. We were waiting for our name to be called to pick up our Indian daughter, Irene.

"This is almost like having a baby!" I exclaimed to my husband. This new addition to our family had just turned eleven and was a fifth-grader in school. Like us, she was new to the Indian Student Placement Program.

The children, who had traveled all night by bus, had arrived two hours earlier and were now being examined by volunteer doctors and dentists to make sure they were all right. "They must be dead tired, poor kids," I thought.

At last, Brother Smith from LDS Social Services, who was handling our placement case, called us into his office. His kind face looked weary.

"I have really been praying these past few weeks," he said, "and have been blessed in finding the right families for all the children."

I thought back to the events that had led us here. First, there was the interview by a stake high councilor, himself a foster parent in the Indian Placement Program for several years. He shared some of the experiences he'd had with his son—some funny, some touching. As foster parents, he explained, we should uphold the standards of the Church and teach our Indian student both by precept and by example. Knowing that we were far from a perfect family was a little frightening, but we did try to live the commandments. Lately, we had been successful in having family prayers and scripture study every day, and we held regular family home evenings.

"Everyone is going to envy us!" our son Ted interjected. "We're going to have so many blessings." Just back from his mission, he knew that to love and serve one another was what the gospel was all about. Our married son, Tom, and his wife, Diana, encouraged us, too.

Then Brother Smith had visited us. "These Indian parents love their children very much," he explained. "They want a better life and education for them. That is why they are able to part with them to let them come on the placement program." We were convinced.

After making the decision, we began to prepare. Our nine-year-old daughter, Pamela, worked diligently readying her room to share with her new sister. She discarded all her "baby things" and cleared out two drawers of her dresser for the new occupant. We went through hand-me-downs from our two older daughters, Jill, then a sixteen-year-old, and Diane, away on a Brigham Young University travel study program in Israel. We found a good pair of pajamas, some T-shirts and pants, and a pretty dress that would do while the weather was still warm. We were ready.

"Here is Irene," announced a teenaged volunteer, breaking my train of thought.

We looked up into the dark eyes of a thin, brown girl. She smiled at us shyly. Her hair was neatly brushed into two long braids. She wore a pair of new jeans, a bright red T-shirt, and a new pair of blue sneakers.

Quickly, we introduced ourselves and I gave her a hug. My husband took the small suitcase from her hand.

From that moment, Pam became Irene's advocate. At home, she showed her where to put her things, which was her bed and her side of the closet. She showed her how things in the house worked—but the telephone was her favorite. It had push buttons.

Pamela introduced her around the neighborhood, and soon Irene had friends.

Although Irene seemed happy with us, she said virtually nothing at first. She would smile and nod or shake her head to our questions, but she didn't speak. On the reservation, she spoke only Navajo, except at school. Since Navajo has a reversed word order, I knew Irene was afraid of making a mistake in front of us. I could empathize with her—I had been to Mexico the summer before and felt very timid in using my limited Spanish to communicate.

Since Irene was too shy to speak, Pam became her mouthpiece. "Irene wants her hair up in rollers for Sunday School." (She had beautiful, thick hair that took a dozen curlers to roll up.) "Irene's still afraid of Daddy." "Irene needs a notebook for school . . . a pair of Sunday School shoes . . ." Several weeks went by and occasionally Irene spoke a few words to me, but none to other family members except her roommate, Pam.

Then one morning an amazing thing happened. It was one of those mornings when everyone was in a grouchy mood because of approaching tests and late nights up studying or working. To make things worse, it seemed that everyone needed rides to different destinations at the same time in the only available car.

Pam announced: "Irene would like to say the prayer this morning." Her eyes were twinkling, and I looked at Irene. Hers were shining, too.

"Would you, Irene?" I asked, incredulously.

She nodded and smiled.

A hush fell over the family. We all bowed our heads, and I could feel the mood of discord change to one of love and caring. Irene spoke slowly, enunciating each word. It was a beautiful, simple prayer, the longest number of words she had ever spoken in our home.

We were touched. There were tears in the eyes of some of us when she was finished. We were bursting with pride.

After the family left for work and school, I went into the room Irene and Pam shared. As usual, their beds were made, their pajamas neatly folded on a chair.

Then I discovered on their dresser a small card. On it, written in imperfect fourth-grade cursive, was the little prayer Irene had just said. In an act of love, Pam had written out the simple prayer to be memorized, spoken before the family and her Heavenly Father, by her sister, Irene.

A Place to Call Home

CHRIS SCHOEBINGER

my parents raised me in the Methodist Church. We were very active members and attended services every week. When I was about thirteen my parents divorced. My dad eventually remarried a woman who was Catholic. My mom also remarried; my new stepdad was Jewish.

And in high school, I met my first Latter-day Saint: Brian. Actually, I didn't know he was a Latter-day Saint until we became best friends. I loved spending time with his family. In fact, conflicts at my own home made me feel a growing love for my new "adopted" family. Brian's parents knew of my situation and invited me to stay with them whenever I wanted. Little did I know that this small gesture of goodwill was literally God's hand in my life. During my senior year of high school, I ended up living with Brian's family for the entire year; it was a place to call home.

After I graduated, Brian and I took a trip to St. George, Utah, to visit his sister in college. I remember the beautiful lights of the St. George Temple. I felt a tug at my spirit and I asked, "What is that building?" We walked around the temple grounds and I felt something very good and pure. My short visit to St. George was life-changing. In fact, that summer I decided to sell my car, move to St. George, and attend Dixie College in the fall. Brian still had a year of high school left, so I went alone.

I moved into a three-bedroom apartment with five other guys. Only one guy was an active member of the LDS church. He was a returned missionary, elders quorum president, and my roommate. We spent many nights talking about religion. My family was still involved in a variety of religions: my brother married a Japanese woman and accepted Buddhism; my sister married into a devout Baptist family; and my cousins, who were "born-again" Christians, kept warning me about the Mormons in Utah.

But I knew the Church was true. After my baptism in March, I realized school would be ending soon. Most college students look forward to summer break, but I was worried. My campus job would end when school did and I was already living from paycheck to paycheck. I lived in the campus dormitory so I would have to find a new place to live. No job, no money, and no place to go. I also wanted to serve a mission, although it seemed highly unlikely I would ever have enough money. I had a year to earn the money, but I also had to earn a living. I wasn't sure what was going to happen, but I trusted that God did. I kept praying and fasting and waiting.

Then one day about a week before school ended, a knock came at my dormitory door. I answered and saw an elderly, white-haired gentleman. He asked, "I'm looking for Chris—is he here?" He seemed pleasant enough, so I nodded. He immediately shouted with joy, stepped into my room, and gave me a big bear hug. I stumbled back as this stranger wrapped his arms around me and squeezed. He said, "I've been looking for you. Your great-grandmother is my aunt, and she told me you were living in St. George, so I just had to come and find you. You can call me Uncle Charles."

In our brief conversation, he told me he was my third cousin and he had felt compelled to find me. Then he asked if I had any place to live for the summer while the dorms were closed. He was delighted to learn I was a member of the Church. So was he. He and his wife had moved to St. George a few years ago. They had an extra room at their home and he invited me to stay with them. But that was only the beginning of Uncle Charles's generosity.

That summer I got a full-time job at the local bookstore, came home to Uncle Charles and his wife, Aunt Margaret, who always had dinner waiting for me, before I left to work the night shift at the movie theaters. When school started again, I kept the bookstore job and went to school full-time. I earned as much money as I could, but Uncle Charles said not to worry, they were planning to support me on my mission. I could hardly believe it. I had a job, savings for my mission, and a place to call home.

During my mission, Uncle Charles and Aunt Margaret wrote me every week. And when I returned to St. George, my room was just the way I left it. They helped me move to Brigham Young University. They let me borrow a car until I could purchase one of my own. They escorted me through the temple, and Uncle Charles was my witness at my temple sealing. They visited after each baby was born, and were a source of spiritual strength and support when I was called as a bishop. I am forever indebted to them for their generosity and kindness. They were truly an answer to my prayers.

Brian called me not too long ago to thank me for my friendship. He thanks *me?* What do you say to someone who blesses your life with the seeds of eternal life? I'm certain God knew what I needed, and so he introduced me to Brian. And like Uncle Charles, he will always have a place in my heart. Someday, I hope I can do the same for someone else—a family member, a friend, someone who is praying, waiting, looking for a place to call home.

A Birthday Gift for the Lord

SPENCER W. KIMBALL

In one of the stakes of Zion lives a family who celebrates a birthday for Jesus. On April 6, 1955, as they gave to me a crisp fifty-dollar bill, they said, "Today is the Lord's birthday. We always give gifts to our family members on their birthdays. We should like to give a gift to the Savior. Will you place this money where it will please the Redeemer most?"

Two days later, Sister Kimball and I were on our way to Europe for a six-months' tour of all the missions. As we made hasty and extensive preparations, we kept thinking about the birthday gift entrusted to us, and then the thought came to us that perhaps in Europe we would find the most appreciative recipient.

For months we toured the missions, held meetings with the missionaries and Saints, and met many wonderful folks. There were numerous opportunities to present the gift, for the majority of the Saints over there could use extra funds. But we waited.

Toward the end of the mission tour we met a little woman in Germany. She was a widow—or was she? She had been alone with her family of children for ten years. Whether her husband was deceased or not she did not know. A victim of World

War II, he had disappeared and no word had ever come from him. It was said that he was behind the Iron Curtain. The little folks who were but children when he was taken away were now nearly grown, and the son was a full-time missionary among his German people.

It was nearing the time of the temple dedication at Bern, Switzerland. I said to this good woman, "Are you going to the temple dedication?" I saw the disappointment in her eyes as she said that she would like to go but how impossible it was because of the lack of finances. "Here is a place for the gift" was the thought that rooted itself in my mind. I quietly checked with the mission president as to her worthiness and the appropriateness of her going to the temple; and then I gave to him half of the gift, which he assured me would pay the actual bus transportation to Bern and return.

A few weeks later we were in southern France. We had driven from Geneva south to the Riviera. The long, circuitous route had taken most of the day. The bumper-to-bumper cars of the crowds of fun-lovers along the beaches delayed us so that for some twenty or thirty miles we moved slowly, inching our way to reach our destination. When we arrived, we were one hour late for our meeting in Nice.

It was a hot night. The building was filled to capacity. A woman sat at the piano, entertaining this large crowd until our arrival. For one hour she had played. I was so embarrassed for our delay and so grateful to her for what she had done to hold the group and entertain them that I inquired concerning her. Her husband, a professor, had died not long before, and the widow was making a meager living through her musical talents. She was a rather recent convert. Her mission president and the elder assured me that she was worthy and deserving, so I left with her mission president, to be given to her, the other half of the Savior's gift.

We completed our mission tours of the ten missions and finally journeyed to Bern for the dedicatory service of the Swiss Temple. The prophet of the Lord, President David O. McKay, was present with three of the Apostles. After the glorious dedication meetings were over, the regular temple services were conducted in the various languages. As I assisted the French Saints in their session, I was conscious that the little musician was there; and she literally beamed as she was enjoying the Savior's birthday gift. She had used it to pay for her transportation to the temple. Her eyes shone with a new luster; her step was lighter; she radiated joy and peace as she came through the temple with new light, new hope. And I whispered to myself, "Thank you, Lord, for good folks who remember the Redeemer on his birthday." . . .

Another year rolled round. Again it was April 6. The birthday family came again. This time it was one hundred dollars. They were pleased with the happiness their gift brought to the recipients. Another birthday gift for the Savior upon his birthday!

Samaritan in Mexico

WENDELL J. ASHTON

I t was a late winter night when my friend Dick [Richard A.] Lambert phoned. He and his wife, Mary, were going to Mexico City. They were going to take along their daughter and four sons, all of them under thirteen. We had made the drive the previous year.

As spring's green began to streak our valley, the Lamberts rolled south toward Mexico. The next two weeks were a wonderland of scenery and sights. They saw the plodding burros everywhere in Mexico, the Mexican men in broad-brimmed straw hats, and the women with their colorful shawls. They saw oxen pulling wooden plows in the fields, and they beheld ancient pyramids and Mexico City's modern skyscrapers, sleek with sweeping walls of concrete, metal, and glass. For days, their eyes had a feast.

Then the two-tone Lambert sedan, of Texas tan and cream, turned northward, toward home. The children were still laughing. They had souvenirs—beautiful leather belts and purses and pocketbooks. They pushed toward Lagos de Moreno, about three hundred miles north of Mexico City. This was in the high, rolling prairie country of central Mexico. A warm sun smiled on the travelers. Mary was now at the wheel.

The car approached a road junction. The signs were in Spanish. Mary's eyes studied the signs a second too long. The big car roared off the highway, spun crazily, and then rolled over three times.

The car stopped upright, a battered heap. Dick was under it, unconscious with a broken nose and foot, five broken teeth, and a generally cut and beaten body. Mary, too, had been hurled from the car, but escaped with minor cuts and bruises. The youngest child, five-year-old Chris, had also been thrown from the car. He, too, was unconscious. The four other children were still in the car. They had no serious hurts.

Almost immediately after the accident, a busload of Mexicans stopped. Some tried to give assistance. With the help of a Mexican motorist, an ambulance, and a truck, the family was taken to Lagos for treatment at the Red Cross station.

Only the wreck that was once a car remained.

Then there drove past the accident scene a middle-aged Mexican couple in a dark sedan. He was a short, rather plump man with graying black hair, and keen, brown eyes. He wore a straw business hat, a short-sleeved sport shirt, and light trousers. His name was Edmundo Martinez G. He was owner of a small ice cream plant in Guadalajara, Mexico's second largest city, about a hundred miles to the west. He was homeward bound from Mexico City.

Edmundo Martinez pressed his brake. Someone had been seriously injured, if not killed, in this accident. His eyes caught the American license plate. That told another tragic story. He knew that the owner of the car, if he survived, would have trouble—much trouble—with customs and with the language. The laws are strict about tourists entering the country with an automobile and leaving without one.

Edmundo Martinez could speak English. He had worked for Henry Ford in

Detroit. He had pressing matters at home in Guadalajara. It was only a few days before the Holy Week, one of the big ice cream seasons of the year in Mexico.

But Edmundo Martinez at the junction took the road to the right, to Lagos, instead of the one to the left, to his home.

He found the Lamberts at the Red Cross station. He gathered the children into his car and took them to the hotel. Little Chris, still unconscious, was with them. The children's new friend rented a room for them and left his wife, who did not speak English, with them. He returned to the hospital, where Dick Lambert's cuts were stitched. Then he drove Dick and Mary to the hotel. He provided the family with dinner. Then he said, "I'm staying in the room right next to yours. Call me if you need me."

Next day, Mr. Martinez drove thirty-three miles to Leon, and there paid the Lamberts' fine—280 pesos (about $25). He boxed up all their belongings and shipped them to Guadalajara. That night he drove all the Lamberts to Guadalajara. Riding in the front seat with him and Mrs. Martinez was Kent, the Lamberts' six-year-old boy, who was almost dark enough to be Mexican. The children sang Sunday School hymns as they rode—that is, all the children but little Chris. He was still unconscious.

Mr. Martinez arranged lodgings for the American family at a Guadalajara hotel. The next morning he took four of them to the hospital for further medical attention. Guadalajara's beautiful blue-lavender jacaranda tree blooms helped brighten that morning. So did the return to consciousness of little Chris.

The Lamberts spent five days in Guadalajara. There was surgery for Chris and a plaster cast for Dick. Edmundo Martinez was always there when he was needed—

in person or on the phone. Daily he brought ice cream for the family. He took their clothes to the cleaners, and he spent a good part of two days clearing red tape with customs.

On the Lamberts' last night before emplaning from Mexico, their friend visited them at the hotel. He handed them forty-eight American dollars and two hundred pesos. "I don't want you to have any trouble getting home," he said. Meanwhile, he had troubles of his own, with the freezing equipment at the plant.

Mary was the last Lambert to say good-bye to Edmundo Martinez. She accompanied him to the hotel elevator. Tears were not far from her bright blue eyes. Her clear, rich voice fought with emotion. "Mr. Martinez," she began, "we want to make it right with you after we return. We can never fully repay you. But what do we owe you in expenses?"

"You don't owe me anything," the Mexican man replied. "Just remember me in your prayers."

With that, he was gone.

The day Dick Lambert arrived home, he mailed a check to his Mexican friend.

Later Edmundo Martinez wrote to the Lamberts. He was still getting papers signed and red tape cleared in connection with their insurance and other matters. "My wife joins me in sending love to all the family," he concluded. "Halo, Kenny [Kent]. Don't forget your friend."

How could anyone forget a friend like Edmundo Martinez G.!

Mother Fed Five Thousand

KAREN CHRISTENSEN LUTHY

there were mornings in Mother's life when she got out of bed with an uncanny desire to "cook for an army." In our early years we children groaned at the prospect of helping her make huge mounds of potato or fruit salad and pans of meatloaf, enchiladas, or Swedish meatballs. Such large quantities of food dulled our appetites for even our favorite dishes.

Mother never could explain the "why" behind her prompting, but those hectic days often ended with welcome, unexpected visits from traveling relatives, friends, and friends of friends who enjoyed all she had prepared. We children came to know that the still, small voice can speak in very practical terms, and that with a trusting response a modern-day "five thousand" could be fed.

However, one Saturday of special preparations passed into Sunday without a visitor. Then, after sacrament meeting, the phone rang and a neighbor's voice said, "Beth, some friends sent a family to stay with us while they go to the temple to be sealed. We haven't room. Have you?"

That was all Mom needed. Five minutes later, as ten strangers pulled into our driveway, we children were setting the table for yet another late Sunday supper.

This time was different, though. In the hustle and bustle Mom spotted one small pair of eyes that seemed to need attention. Her welcoming words to the family were, "Let's get that boy to a doctor."

Dad called a good friend—an eye specialist—who identified a burrowing spore that, he said, would have caused permanent blindness if it had been left untreated any longer.

How thankful we were that even in the midst of confusion Mother had heard and heeded the still, small voice.

Later that night after the family was bedded down, Mother discovered her next challenge. Laundering our guests' clothes in preparation for the important day ahead, she found that most of the shirts and blouses had not been strong enough to survive one last washing.

Then came a frantic inventory of our closets, late-night calls to neighbors, and an early-morning collection of beautiful, donated clothes. I'll always remember the pride in Mother's eyes as she sent those parents and their eight children to the temple to be sealed, "never looking better."

We learned later that this family had saved money for their temple trip by living in the back of a large truck.

That family retained a special membership in Mom's "five thousand," as did one of our neighbors, Ern, who lived in a one-room shack. For years his life was a mystery to us, although we knew that he had long been inactive in the Church. Perhaps his inactivity was due partially to his hunched back—the result of a poorly repaired bone fracture—or perhaps it was due to his lack of teeth, or his Word of Wisdom problems. Mom, though, prompted by that still, small voice, helped bring about a major change in his life.

For a long time, Ern declined our dinner invitations. Then Mom, aware of his sensitivity over his lack of teeth, started sending Sunday dinner to his home where he could eat comfortably and privately.

But that was not his real "feeding." That came later in the week when he returned the dishes. Then, when invited to visit, he would spend most of a leisurely afternoon talking while Mom worked and the younger children played around him. Other relationships developed, and in two years Ern cheerfully exchanged his usual seat on a bench in front of the courthouse for a seat in the temple, doing endowment work. But he always reserved one afternoon each week to return his dishes and visit with Mom in the kitchen.

Such experiences over the years proved to us that Mom's desire to "cook for an army" was really the work of an inspired and generous heart. Ern described her as "a mighty fine woman." She had the capacity to see that people needed not only food for their bodies, but food for their spirits, too.

"Take Whatever You Need"

WENDY McKINNEY

My grandfather, F. Elmer Foutz, was a captain in the 8th Engineer Battalion, a part of the First Cavalry Division, during the Korean War.

When Captain Foutz was in Tokyo at the end of his tour of duty, he stayed at a relatively quiet hotel on the outskirts of town. On a return trip to the hotel on a crowded streetcar, as he stood with his arms full of purchases, someone picked his pocket and stole all his money (more than $100) and his identification. The hotel required payment in advance each night, and now he didn't have any money to pay the bill. He tried to explain to the desk clerk what had happened, and though the clerk wasn't very sympathetic, he finally let Captain Foutz up to his room.

Captain Foutz needed to raise some money in order to travel back to town to get a new identification pass from military headquarters and to cash a check at the PX. He decided to take a roll of colored film, which was always in demand, down to the recreation room in the basement of the hotel to see if he could sell it.

On the way down the hall he met a big African American sergeant who was looking for Captain Foutz. When my grandfather identified himself as Captain Foutz, the sergeant explained that he had been standing behind Captain Foutz at the hotel front desk. He overheard the captain's predicament and decided to help. The sergeant held out his billfold filled with ten-dollar bills and told Captain Foutz to take whatever he needed. Grandfather took a ten-spot, thanked the sergeant profusely, and got his name and unit in Korea. When he got back to his outfit, he wrote to the sergeant's commanding officer and related the story, asking him to please do this man a favor if he ever had the chance. He also enclosed a ten-dollar bill to pay his debt.

Advice from a Pro

RICHARD EYRE

i was coaching a "bitty basketball team" of kids aged five to seven which included two of our boys. A new boy joined the team just before one of the games. His parents dropped him off and left him with us. As a crowd of spectators assembled and the gym became noisy, the new boy started to cry and to say that he didn't want to play. I did all I could to encourage him, but he was afraid. The best I could do was to get him to quiet down and sit on the bench and watch, with the assurance that he wouldn't have to play unless he wanted to.

A little later I noticed my five-year-old, who had been taken out of the game, sitting with and talking to the new boy. I angled myself closer on the bench so I could hear. Our boy was saying, "I felt a little scared the first time, too, because there's so many people, but I got used to it, and now it's fun. Don't worry, you'll get used to it, too."

Five Lessons of Love

ELAINE CANNON

i once had to shut myself and our four little ones under six into the nursery in our home. I had a fever of 104 degrees, and I was pregnant again. Staying upright was no longer a viable option. In my misery I curled up on a youth bed to keep a watchful eye on our precious destroying angels. Balls and baby bottles sailed over my head while dark thoughts stirred my mind. My young husband was a conscientious new bishop who was always visiting the sick, and I wondered how sick we had to be to get the bishop to come and call in our home!

I didn't feel like much of a mother—more like a big baby, such was my self-pity.

Then the doorbell rang, and I dragged myself from the bed to peer through the window to the front porch. There stood the Relief Society president, an older woman who worked closely with my young husband in the welfare needs of our ward. She was old enough to be my mother, and I was appalled that she should catch me in my failure, in this house of chaos where no mother's hand had been raised recently to do more than keep the little ones from hurting each other.

The stampede to answer the doorbell came from children aching for release from the confinement of the nursery. While I called through the window that I was ill and would see her another time, the children were already opening the door for her.

Then the most marvelous bit of "other mothering" occurred. This time I was the child being taught lifesaving lessons. This fine friend explained that she had been driving by our house and had felt prompted by the Spirit that help was needed therein.

Lesson one: Be in tune and respond to the promptings of the Spirit.

She had hurried home to get her ever-ready Friendship Bag, full of supplies and surprises for the sick and afflicted.

Lesson two: Be prepared and equipped to meet the need.

Returning to our home, she rang the doorbell until there was a response.

Lesson three: Don't give up too soon in doing your good deeds!

She told me to lie down on the living room couch while she lured the children to the kitchen table with cookies and new coloring books. She would help me in a moment. In relief, I obeyed.

Lesson four: Even a mother needs a mother on occasion.

Sister Jensen took my foot in her hands, ignoring my protests of embarrassment that she would be doing that to *me*! She talked quietly and comfortingly, all the while massaging each foot while she healed my soul. There was quiet for a moment, and then I got lesson five: *"Love your partner, Elaine. Love him enough so that he has plenty to give his ward members. Let your bishop-husband be a good shepherd."*

"What a Dinner We Had That Day"
HANNAH CORNABY

One morning having, as usual, attended to family prayer, in which, with greater significance than is often used, we asked, "Give us this day our daily bread," and having eaten a rather scanty breakfast—every morsel we had in the house— Edith was wondering what we should have for dinner and why Pa had not sent us some fish. I too was anxious, not having heard from Provo for some days; so, telling my darling I would go and see if Sister Ellen Jackson (whose husband was also one of the fishing party) had heard any news, I started off. Sister Jackson had not heard from the fishery but was quite cheerful, telling me how well her garden was growing, adding that the radishes were fit for use, and insisting that I must have some. It was good to see something to eat; and, quite pleased, I bade her good morning. I passed on my way the house of Brother Charles Gray, and Sister Gray asked me where I had gotten such fine radishes. I told her and offered to divide them with her, to which she agreed, providing I would take in exchange some lettuce and cress, of which she had plenty. She filled a pan with these, and I hurried away thinking how pleased my children would be, if only we had bread to eat with them.

As I was passing Brother Simon Baker's house, Sister Baker saw me and invited me in. I told her I had left my children and could not stop long. She then asked me where I had gotten such nice green stuff, and when I told her and offered her some, she replied, "If I could exchange some for butter, I would be glad." She then gave me a piece of nice fresh butter, which had just come from their dairy on the Jordan, and also a large slice of cheese. If I only had bread, I thought, how good these would be! Just then my eyes rested upon a large vessel full of broken bread. Sister Baker, seeing I had noticed it, told me its history. It had been sent the day before, in a sack, to the canyon where her husband had a number of men working. On the way it had fallen from the wagon and been crushed under the wheel. She did not know what to do with it, remarking that she would offer me some of it but feared I would feel insulted, although she assured me it was perfectly clean. I accepted her offer, and, after filling a large pan, she sent her daughter home with me to carry it.

The children were watching for my return, and when they saw the bread, they clapped their hands with delight. Bread, butter, cheese, radishes, lettuce, and cress! What a dinner we had that day! Elijah never enjoyed the dinner the ravens brought him more than I did that meal; nor did he more fully understand that a kind Providence had furnished it.

The Extra Ham

R I C H A R D   M O O R E

When my wife and I were first married we lived in a basement apartment in Provo. I was still going to school and working part-time. My wife dropped out of school for a while to help support us as I finished school. There was very little money to cover all of the expenses.

My parents lived about a half hour away from us, and we used to drop by once in a while to visit and to get something to eat. During one of those early visits my dad took me aside and said, "I went shopping the other day and accidentally bought an extra case of soup. Our food storage area is pretty filled up and we have no place to put this case of soup. We really can't use it and I don't know what to do with it. Could you take it?"

"Sure," I replied. "I'm happy to be able to help."

We took the soup and I was pleased twofold. We got some food we could use and I was able to help out my dad. A few weeks later on another visit my dad had made another shopping error and we went home with a number of items that wouldn't fit in his freezer. This went on from time to time until I was beginning to worry about my dad. Perhaps my mom should do all the shopping. Dad didn't seem to be able to handle it very well.

Around Easter we traveled to my parents' home for a family get-together. When we were getting ready to go back to the apartment my dad took me aside and said, "I came home from the supermarket the other day with an extra ham. We've already got the one so we don't need it. Could you and Lani use a ham?"

Well, I'm no dummy. You can only fool me for five to seven months. Extra case-lot items are one thing, but who would accidentally buy one too many hams? "Sure, we'd love to take the ham," I said, and then with a look that would let him know that I knew what he was up to, I added, "Now, how much do I owe you?"

"You don't understand, I'm giving it to you."

"I understand completely," I said, taking out my wallet. "Let me pay you back."

He paused for a couple of seconds, looked at me, and said, "You can't possibly pay me back."

I was just thinking that must be some expensive ham when my dad clarified, "It's not just the ham or the soup or the other things we've given you. It's all the things over the years that your mom and I have done for you. It's the sacrifice, and time, and energy, and money, and worries that we have invested in you. You will never be able to pay us back for all we've done for you."

My father is not the kind of guy that fishes for compliments or appreciation and I was pretty sure he wasn't asking me to pay him back on some kind of monthly installment plan. Because he doesn't normally talk this way, I knew he was serious and was trying to make a point. But if there was no way I could ever pay Mom and him back, what could I do?

It was like he read my mind. "The only thing you can do to pay me back," he said, "is to someday do things to help your own kids. I'm not only doing things for you and your sisters because I love you, but through you I'm also paying back your grandpa and grandma for everything they did for me. That's the way it works."

Since having my own children I have realized that my dad was right. That *is* the way it works.

The Neighbor Plate

BETTY G. SPENCER

The well-worn, deep metal pie plate didn't look like anything valuable as it lay neglected in a kitchen drawer. An outsider would have quickly discarded it as something of little value, but to our family . . . it represented a cherished characteristic of a friendly, vivacious grandmother.

The pie plate was what we called Grandmother's Neighbor Plate, and it was one of her most often used kitchen utensils.

Grandmother always seemed to make a little extra whenever she prepared a special treat for her family. Somehow, the extra was placed in the pie plate and carried to an appreciative friend or neighbor. When sickness, trouble, or death visited a neighborhood home, the pie plate inevitably was carried to the kitchen door, and the sorrowing family members were cheered by the delectable contents.

Grandmother, an excellent cook, was locally famous for her flaky pie crusts, mouthwatering fruitcakes, and feathery light hot rolls.

The Neighbor Plate helped Grandmother get acquainted with a newcomer, too. Moving day was sure to find her running over with a "little something" to help out with the first meal in the new home. We soon noticed that the Neighbor Plate was an important link in the close, warm friendships that grew along her street.

Frequently the plate was returned heaped with apples, berries, pieces of newly baked cake, or other special treats from grateful hearts. Gratitude delighted Grandmother, but those few neighbors who felt duty-bound to return the favor were a genuine disappointment. Grandmother felt that her offering should be savored, enjoyed—even appreciated—but not necessarily paid back.

Grandmother is gone now, but the philosophical values she implanted in our hearts are with us still.

Her daughters have remained in the same friendly mountain valley where they grew to womanhood, but the grandchildren have settled across the country from Florida to California. Our homes are as varied as we are, but each of us has an important piece of kitchen equipment. We would never think of keeping house without a Neighbor Plate!

Our grandmother's philosophy of giving is as appropriate today as it was fifty years ago. What we give is not really too important. It may be lemon meringue pie in Florida or Hungarian goulash in California. Whatever else we may add, love and friendliness are the most important ingredients that are ever offered on a Neighbor Plate!

An Unsigned Note

MARY ELLEN EDMUNDS

We have many opportunities and assignments to offer our love in person, but some of the most interesting reactions occur when we share it anonymously. One night I returned home exhausted from a long shift at the hospital. My shift as evening nursing supervisor was to have ended around 11:30 P.M., but so much had happened and was still happening that I didn't get home until well after midnight. My white Clinic shoes weighed a hundred pounds each as I started up the stairs. And then I saw them: the flowers. A beautiful collection of colors wrapped in cellophane, waiting for me at the top of the stairs by my door.

It's hard to describe the happy feeling that came into my heart as I looked at the flowers and wondered why someone had given them to me. There was a little card with my name on the envelope. As I reached for it I was already thinking, "Oh, what can I do for them?" (As if we need to get even when someone does something kind for us.)

I got the flowers into my apartment and sat down to look at the card, wondering, "Who is it? Who did this kind thing for me?" The card said something like this: "Thank you, Mary Ellen, for being such a good friend. I appreciate your kindness and help. I love you." *And it wasn't signed!* Anonymous! Now what? How can you thank people if they don't tell you who they are?

Some interesting things happened to me. First, I went to bed thinking that someone loved me. Someone cared about me. Can we ever get too much of that? Second, I was going a little crazy. Who had done this? How could I say thanks and get it over with? Now I'd have to be nice to *everyone*—at least until the flowers died.

Finally, I began trying to decide who had done such a nice thing. Who would have given me such a wonderful surprise? Interestingly, virtually everyone I knew and some I didn't know got onto my list of possibilities. Everyone in my family was on that list, and everyone at the hospital. When I arrived at work the next day and was making my rounds, I realized I was being very friendly, smiling a lot, greeting everyone with an extra effort to be genuinely interested. I'm sure some thought, "What's with Edmunds?"

As a result of that anonymous gift of love, I looked at everyone differently. Each person I saw might have been the one who had done such a nice thing for me. It was as if I took a new look at everyone I knew and found in them a kindness that I hadn't thought about or acknowledged nearly often enough.

Helping Hands

FLO WHITTEMORE

I had not invited her to come into my home that morning. . . . Yet, at nine o'clock, there she was, energetically scrubbing away on my dirty woodwork and looking as cheerful, I thought to myself, as though she enjoyed it.

Why? I questioned almost aloud as I watched her from the davenport where I was lying. Then, as if an effort to discover why was too much exertion for a body weakened by illness and a mind weary of trying to solve problems, I said a bit querulously to myself, Oh, well, if she *wants* to do it, it's perfectly all right! Only I don't see why she should *enjoy* doing it!

She was our very capable, very much loved Relief Society president. When I had answered her knock on my door that eventful day, she had smiled pleasantly as she asked, "How are you this morning?"

Glad to have anyone come in, I quickly bade her enter. But before I could tell her of my aches and pains and discouragement, she said, "I think you'd better just lie down again and take it easy. You've been pretty sick, you know. I didn't have anything in particular to do today, so I thought I'd just slip in here and wash your woodwork and clean your windows for you. I know it must be hard to lie there and look at these things that need doing."

All of a sudden, a spark of interest stirred inside me. "It will be nice," I acknowledged, "to have the windows washed, especially this one in front of me. It's so dirty, everything looks gray outside."

"I know. Almost gives you a gloomy outlook on life, doesn't it?" she replied cheerily as she proceeded to undo the bundle of cloths she had brought.

Hmmm! I thought, *almost!* Why shouldn't I be altogether gloomy just lying here day after day? And I retired again into my morbid thoughts. . . .

I became fascinated as I watched her quick, vigorous movements: up and down and across, not a stroke wasted. Lola was like that in everything she did. Without saying a word, she radiated life and good cheer. Deftly, almost gracefully, I thought, she bent to wring the water out of the scrub cloth as she wiped the clean white wood with clear water before polishing it with a dry cloth.

We didn't talk; I was too tired. But it seemed to me only a matter of few minutes until all the woodwork in the living room was spotless.

"It does look better," I acknowledged aloud. "I didn't realize it was so dingy."

"Well, with a coal fire, it doesn't take long," Lola answered as she picked up the pans of dirty water. Then, stepping quickly into the kitchen, she got a smaller pan of clean water and soap and returned to the living room window. . . .

In a very short while she had both of the windows and the glass in the door so clean and shining that one could almost believe there was no glass in the frames at all!

For the first time since she had come, I think I smiled, and something deep down inside me fluttered ever so slightly. I felt it but ignored it.

If Lola was disappointed, she gave no sign; but resolutely filling her pans with clean, warm water, she began scrubbing the woodwork in the bedroom, all the while whistling or humming a cheery accompaniment to the rhythmic movements of her hands. . . .

As Lola prepared to leave, I got up to thank her. I expressed appreciation for her efforts to help me, and I was glad to have my house clean, too.

"It was nice of you to do it," I said. And then, as she chatted happily about making some bright ruffled curtains for the kitchen windows, the miracle happened.

I glanced down at her hands that must have been lovely when she came to my house that morning. I could see that they were small and beautifully shaped with tapering fingers that looked more like they should be skimming over piano keys than scrubbing dirty woodwork.

But now they were red, rough, and scratched, the nails cracked and broken . . . but before I could say a word, Lola was gone. . . .

I knew she did not have to do the menial tasks that she had done so *willingly* in my home. It was for me—to help lift me up out of the discouragement and despair into which I had fallen and to give me a new hold on life. For *love of me,* she had scrubbed and scoured, not caring for a moment what was happening to her hands. They looked so sore, they must have hurt her, but there was no word of complaint— just song!

At that moment, it was as though a spring shower had suddenly descended upon my spirit and was cleansing it of all the accumulation of doubt and despair and weakness that had piled up during months of illness.

A Visiting Teacher for Jennifer

CATHY BLAISDELL

Jennifer is my oldest daughter. She is 32 and has severe mental and physical handicaps. She lives at home with us and goes to a day-training facility each weekday. The bus picks up Jennifer in her wheelchair in the morning and brings her home each afternoon. We don't take Jennifer to church any more, but we used to.

Jennifer does not walk or talk. Because she has the developmental level of a nine-month-old, when she was Primary age she seemed to fit best in the nursery on Sundays. Each Sunday she sat on the carpeted floor in the nursery and happily played with the toys. My husband was in the bishopric, and there were younger children in our family to take care of in church. When Jennifer was about thirteen, I realized she was too big and too old for the nursery anymore. There was no other place for her, though, so she stayed home on Sundays. Even though Jennifer was on the attendance rolls of the Primary and Young Women and eventually Relief Society, mostly she was overlooked by ward members.

I felt badly that Jennifer was missing out on the spiritual aspects of Sunday, and I tried to fill that void by playing cassette tapes of Primary songs and singing to her.

For my son's Eagle Scout project, his troop recorded books on tape that Jennifer could listen to.

Our ward boundaries changed, and we went to a new ward with a new bishop. Jennifer's birthday is five days before Christmas, and Bishop Murray came to see Jennifer on her birthday. He spoke to her as if she understood his words, and he treated her like she was an important person.

The sun was shining on a bright spring morning. I was cleaning up the kitchen after breakfast when the doorbell interrupted my work. It was Floy Murray, the bishop's wife, and we chatted in my kitchen. Floy kindly said to me, "Jennifer needs a visiting teacher, and I would like to be her visiting teacher." Spontaneously, tears trickled down my cheeks. Floy said if it was all right with me she would call the Relief Society president and make the arrangements. I was overwhelmed that someone would see a need and want to visit Jennifer.

For years Floy came at least once each month to visit Jennifer: balloons on Jennifer's birthday, pictures for Jennifer's bedroom, treats to eat, and always a lesson. Floy often reminded me, "Jennifer's spirit is not handicapped." Between visits in our home, Floy called to see how we were.

Visiting teaching assignments change, and even though Floy is no longer Jennifer's official visiting teacher, Floy still brings balloons on Jennifer's birthday, asks her how school is, and is an important part of Jennifer's life. Jennifer squeals with delight when she hears Floy's voice.

I have a new understanding of the scripture, "Inasmuch as ye have done it unto one of the least of these . . . , ye have done it unto me" (Matthew 25:40). When Jennifer's life is blessed, so is mine.

My Father and Blind John

DENNIS K. ALLEN

i first remember him at fifty years old, tall and strong. He dressed in bib overalls and heavy work shoes and wore dark glasses all the time. A friend of my father's, he lived alone but worked for us at times. I remember that he carried his head cocked to one side and let it nod up and down—Dad said it helped him to hear better. His name was John, and he was over forty years blind.

Blind John lived in an unfinished, rustic one-room house with a very crooked chimney. The house was untidy and smelled of musty bedding and clothes, fried food, smoked bacon, coffee grounds, and coal and wood smoke. John had built the house—that accounted for the crooked walls and chimney. He ate mostly bacon and eggs, fried potatoes, bread and milk—that accounted for the smell.

Although John's house was about a mile and a half from our house, and about the same distance from the service station (the only place for John to buy food), he could walk those gravel roads with a stride that my young legs envied.

He did minor carpentry work for people in town if they weren't too particular about the finished product. One summer he worked with my dad to build the structure that became a service station. John would walk to our house, work with my dad during the day, eat sandwiches my mother prepared while he sat on a pile of boards or a wagon tongue, and then walk back to his home that night. There may have been times when Dad took him home with a team and wagon or later in the car, when we had one, but I can't remember it. I only remember John walking home and Dad watching until he was out of sight.

Dad drove a school bus during the school season and would pass John's house four times a day. He would honk the bus horn, the school kids would wave, and John would wave back as if he could see the students' faces. When John would oversleep and not be at the little dark window, or if there wasn't smoke coming out of the crooked chimney, Dad would stop and holler from the bus doorway, "John, how are you going to get things done if you sleep until noon?" John would come to the window and make some excuse about his alarm clock, and Dad would leave.

In retrospect, the way my father managed his communications with John has built a lasting appreciation in my mind for my father. Dad didn't read the works of great psychologists, attend lectures, or listen to tapes. He just used common sense and sensitivity. He checked on John almost daily, but I never remember him asking: "John, are you all right? Is there anything I can do for you? Do you need anything? Can I take you somewhere? Can I shovel your snow?"

Instead, Dad would ask such questions as "John, I've been preparing a 'reading.' Would you listen and see what you think?"

"John, I'm going to be putting up this building, or building this fence. What do you think of the idea? Could you help me with it?"

"What have you heard new on your *Reader's Digest* records? Those are good ideas; I'll write them down. Can I use your typewriter?"

Dad always asked for help from blind John, and he always got help; but in truth Dad was not getting—he was giving. In all he did with John, his message was "You are a person, you are important, your opinion means something, you have a right to be here; poverty is temporary and unimportant; dignity is eternal and essential."

In those days, when you could no longer take care of yourself, you went into an "old folks' home." At age seventy-one and ill, John decided to make the move, but it was not a defeat. There he regained his health and met a happy woman whom he called Sunshine. He shared his strong arms and legs with a lady who had never walked; she shared her eyes with a man who couldn't see. John changed his lifestyle, became reconverted to the Church, was married in the Logan Temple, and lived a new and different life for thirteen years before he and his companion passed away. No one was happier for John during those last years than my dad.

Love and concern and independence. My dad, and blind John.

A Change in Routine

KATHLEEN "CASEY" NULL

a change in routine. That's what I thought I needed.
And I got it, and then some. But it wasn't quite what I had in mind.
Within a little over a week,

- my car broke down—water pump.

- I developed an allergy to my contact lens solution.

- I came down with strep throat, and it felt like hot coals when I tried to swallow.
I quit using the phone when a friend thought I was a crank caller and hung up on me.

- the optometrist took away my lenses and left me in a blur.

- the plumbing backed up and flooded three carpeted rooms and my side of the closet.

- I broke out in hives from the antibiotics I was taking for strep throat.

- I came down with a sniffly virus.

- the doctor put me on a powerful antihistamine, and I developed a tendency to fall asleep in the middle of the day during my four children's activities.

So there I was, splotchy, itchy, car-less, drugged senseless, sniffly, blind, and trying to cope in a swampland.

Pathos was not my idea of a change in routine.

I sank onto the couch feeling helplessly resigned to my fate, and my three-year-old, normally preoccupied with his needs, came and stroked my hair. "It's all right, Mommy, I'll take care of you," he said soothingly.

He brought me one of his blankets and a book. He tucked the blanket around me and handed me the book to read to him.

It was a child's book about the universe. We spent a quiet period lost in the solar system, marvelling over the way it was organized and ordered for us. My voice began to get a little choked up.

There wasn't anything on those pages that I didn't already know from somewhere, but I was overwhelmed at the beauty and awesomeness of it all and at Him who organized it so precisely. My son looked up at me and patted my splotchy cheek. "It's all right, Mom."

Yes, I thought, it certainly is.

"Here's Your Paper, Mister"

GEORGE BERGSTROM

the first time I met Jimmy Leaver*, he was selling newspapers on the corner of Fourth Street and Broadway in Santa Monica. It was just before the Great Depression and I was on my way home from work. As I reached the intersection, he approached me eagerly and flashed a quick smile that beamed right into my heart from his grimy face.

"Here's your paper, mister. Paper!" he said, as he thrust the *Evening Outlook* into my hand. I could not resist his appeal. I took the paper and gave him a coin. He beamed me one more smile of thanks and dashed across the street to sell another paper.

This boy was a ragamuffin if there ever was one. His freckled face was dirty, and his head was covered with uncut, tousled hair the color of straw. His toes stuck out of holes in canvas shoes laced with pieces of string.

His soiled corduroy trousers were frayed at the bottoms and torn at the knees. His shirt was buttonless and tucked carelessly into the top of his pants, one side

*His name has been changed.

flapping in the breeze as he ran. His pants were held up by a piece of string instead of a belt. He looked as though he had never seen soap and water. . . .

I thought about him all the way home. In spite of his appearance, I was strangely attracted to him. I tried to analyze why. I knew I felt sorry for him, but my feelings went deeper than that. I felt we were kindred spirits—he was a child of God, the same as I was. And he needed my help.

The thought appealed to me. I have always enjoyed working with boys. In fact, I was working with them at the time, both in Scouting and in the Church. I had great faith in boys and their inherent goodness. This boy kept popping up in my mind. I had the urge to do something for him, not exactly to test my faith but rather to put faith into action.

By five o'clock the next day I had worked out a tentative plan. After work I again walked down Fourth Street. The boy was there. Again I bought a paper. This time as he approached I gave him a smile, and as he handed me a paper, I said, "What is your name, sonny?"

He accepted the coin I gave him before he replied, "Jimmy."

"Jimmy who?"

His eyes were constantly searching the street for customers. "Jimmy Leaver."

In a voice as warm and friendly as I could make it, I said, "How old are you, Jimmy?"

He looked me squarely in the eye, hesitated slightly, then answered, "I'm twelve. Why?"

"Well, I like you, Jimmy, and I'm interested in you. Do you mind if I ask you a few questions?"

He countered with, "What about? Are you with the cops?"

"No, of course not, nothing like that," I assured him. "Tell me, Jimmy, where do you live?"

He pointed vaguely to the north. "On Tenth Street."

This was not too specific, but I let it pass.

Jimmy was again anxiously scanning the street for other customers and probably looking for an excuse to get away. As soon as I had his attention again I gave him a level look and said, "Jimmy, how would you like to be a Boy Scout?"

He looked at me as if he could hardly believe his ears. Then, before he answered, he glanced down at his ragged clothing. He spoke in a bantering tone. "In these clothes—are you kidding? That's a laugh." But I had seen a gleam in his eyes; he wanted to be a Scout. I had caught his interest, though he tried not to show it.

I knew I would have to do some fast thinking to sell myself to this lad. He was plenty sharp. But if I was going to make the sale, it had to be now.

With all the sincerity I could muster, I said, "Jimmy, clothes don't make a Scout; it's what a boy has in his heart that counts. By the way, we're having our troop meeting tonight at the Grant School. Come along and join us. We always have a lot of fun. And don't worry about your clothes—come as you are."

He looked at me with a quizzical expression in his blue eyes, sizing me up and down, and then he asked, "Are you the Scoutmaster?"

"Sure," I answered, "I'm the Scoutmaster of Troop Ten. We're a new troop with about fifteen boys, all about your age. We go camping, hiking, cook our own meals, learn signaling, first aid, and lots of other things boys like to do. In a couple of weeks we're going to Camp Trefoil for an overnight camp. How about coming along as my guest? What do you say?"

He did not answer immediately. He paused, as though trying to make up his mind. Then he said, "Well, maybe, if I don't forget. Do I have to get my mom's permission?"

"Yes, of course. The main thing is not to forget the Scout meeting tonight at 7:30 at the Grant School. Remember, I'll be looking for you." With this remark I strode off.

Well, Jimmy came to the meeting that night all right. He had washed his hands and face and tried to comb his unruly hair. Otherwise, his appearance was no different than it had been earlier that day.

It was a good Scout meeting. I had planned it well, and the program included many things boys like to do. Jimmy entered into it wholeheartedly. No one could run faster or yell louder. He had the time of his life.

After the meeting I said to Jimmy, "Wait for me, and I'll take you home." He tried to talk me out of it, but I insisted. I really wanted to find out where he lived and why he was so cagey about it. I also wanted to meet his parents.

When we arrived at Tenth and Arizona, he directed me to let him off at the alley in the middle of the block, explaining that he wanted to go in the back way. As I stopped the car, he gave me a quick handshake, a thanks, a goodnight; and he was gone. I saw him open a gate in the middle of the block and disappear.

The next day I returned to the area and had no trouble finding the place where Jimmy lived. It was neither his home nor his family. The home belonged to an elderly couple who had told Jimmy's mother they would try to help him. However, there was no room for Jimmy in the house, so he had to sleep in a large packing box in the backyard. This had been his home for over a year. To say that I was shocked would be an understatement.

From the old couple I obtained the address of Jimmy's mother. She was working for a family in the Brentwood area. I went to see her. She was a wisp of a woman and very reluctant to talk about the past. Finally I was able to convince her that I had no ulterior motives; I only wanted to help her and Jimmy, if she would let me. During the course of several visits, the whole story unfolded. Briefly, it was something like this:

Jimmy came from a broken home. The last time he had seen his father was when he was about six years old. He was told only that his father had gone away.

The truth was that Jimmy's father was serving a life sentence in San Quentin prison, and Jimmy's older brother had been involved with the police for robbery and other crimes; he was now in a reform school. Jimmy's mother was broken in health, but she lived with this family, working for her board and room. There was no room for Jimmy, so he had been shifting for himself. This was the situation the night Jimmy came to his first Scout meeting.

I became very busy in Jimmy's behalf. In a few days I found a family living in the better part of town who invited him to come and live with them and to share a room with one of their boys who was about the same age as Jimmy. From a Scouting family came an assortment of clothing for Jimmy, including several pairs of leather shoes.

These outfits and a haircut made Jimmy look like a different boy. And he began to feel like a different boy—as if he was wanted and belonged to someone. During this time, I saw Jimmy every day. The summer passed quickly.

In September Jimmy went back to school. He soon adjusted to his adopted family, sharing in the chores of the home and doing his part. On Sundays he attended church with his mother, and gradually his whole way of life changed.

One night he came to Scout meeting in a brand new Scout uniform. He said he had found it on his bed, and it had his name on it. It was just the right size. All the insignia were sewn on in the right places. This was the turning point in Jimmy's life. He wore his new uniform everywhere he went.

From that time on he began to take personal pride in his appearance. The uniform became a symbol, and Jimmy was now on the trail to citizenship. A contact was made with the *Evening Outlook,* and Jimmy was offered a paper route and a steady income, which he accepted with much satisfaction. I helped him find a used bicycle, which he needed for the job and could pay for out of his earnings.

Finally, Jimmy's mother was helped to secure a position with another family, where the work was easier; and there was also a spare room for Jimmy, who went to live with his mother for the first time in nearly two years.

As Jimmy's life became stabilized, his attitude and conduct changed. He began to assert himself. He was a natural leader and developed rapidly. He advanced in the ranks of Scouting as fast as time permitted. . . .

I became "uncle" to Jimmy. It was more than an affectionate term; I acted as his adopted dad. . . .

In every way my faith in him was justified, and in everything he took me into his confidence. When he bought his first new bicycle, I cosigned the purchase agreement;

when he graduated from Lincoln Junior High School, I was there; when he received his Eagle badge at a court of honor, I was there, and so was his mother. As she pinned the Eagle badge on his uniform she cried, but her tears were of joy, not sorrow. For now she knew that she had a son she could be proud of.

Two years later Jimmy graduated from Santa Monica High School at the head of his class. I marveled at what had happened in four short years!

But the crowning achievement came when Jimmy rented an apartment so that he and his mother could live together. He vowed that she would never have to work again as long as she lived. And she never did.

That was forty years ago. Today Jimmy is a responsible citizen and a successful businessman. He was not satisfied with just graduating from high school; he put himself through college. He has a master's degree from the University of Southern California. He is now a leader in one of California's biggest industries. He is a Rotarian, a churchman, and a leader in the community in which he lives. He has two married sons and two daughters.

Cow for Sale

LYNN C. JAYNES

Several years ago my sister, Jane, and I inherited a wringer-type mop bucket. We were next-door neighbors, so sharing the bucket was a simple matter of organizing our cleaning days. Although we both had young families, lived on farms, and had large linoleum floors that needed frequent mopping, we didn't have any problems getting the bucket back and forth. She knew where I stored the bucket and I knew where she stored it, so we just helped ourselves on mop day.

Jane and I shared other things, too. I borrowed her bread pans on baking day, and she borrowed the pressure cooker during canning season. We planted gardens side by side and raised chickens in the same pen. We used each other's lawn mowers and fed each other's children. She taught my children piano lessons. When her three-year-old daughter "ran away" to my house, I assigned the little girl some work that was harder than usual—and she was soon ready to go back home.

We cried when changes in our husbands' employment separated us. Tearfully, we divvied up our wares. I knew I would miss her greatly.

About a year later, we were thrilled to be neighbors again. By that time, she had a pressure cooker and I had bought my own bread pans. I got to keep the mop bucket because Jane's new house was mostly carpeted. That's when we bought the five hundred-dollar milk cow.

I don't even recall now who bought the cow first. But our arrangement was for one family to milk her in the mornings and the other family to take care of her at night. The cow gave enough milk to supply both families, and we raised calves besides.

Through the years, both families occasionally had financial struggles. I remember a time when taxes came due for my sister's family. They were short about five hundred dollars. At that time, they owned the cow. So we bought the cow from them, and they were able to pay their taxes. Meanwhile, they still milked mornings, we still milked evenings, and nothing really changed.

Then one day we needed funds to pay medical bills. My sister and her husband bought back the cow.

I guess we've lost track now of how many times the cow has been bought and sold, but during these ownership shuffles, the cow has never even changed pastures or had her milking routine interrupted. As far as I could see, there was never any real advantage to ownership. Sometimes we had to concentrate to even figure out who the current owner was.

And Jane seemed to agree. One day as ownership was changing hands again, she remarked, "This is silly that we pass this cow back and forth and declare 'ownership' as if it really meant something. We ought to just give each other the money whenever it's needed." We laughed about it and dubbed the animal our consecration cow.

Awhile back the pump in our well broke. A new one was going to cost a fair bit, and my husband and I were trying to decide how to pay for it when the phone rang. It was my sister.

"I can't believe your pump went out! Listen, do you need us to buy the cow?"

I smiled. It didn't even matter that they already owned her.

"The Sky Is Blue Again"

SYLVIA PROBST YOUNG

On a day in late autumn, when the clouds hung oppressively low and a mournful wind cried through the bare, brown trees, I closed my door and walked hurriedly across the field to the home of a friend. My thoughts as I walked along were dark as the day. I was lonely, disappointed, sick at heart, feeling that life had hurt me more than I could bear. Nothing seemed really worthwhile anymore. I needed to talk to someone—I wanted sympathy, and so I went to see a woman who is my friend.

She was in her little garden behind the house, digging some carrots for the soup she was making.

"It's the kind of day for good, homemade vegetable soup," she exclaimed, after greeting me warmly. "Come in. I have a nice fire and we can talk."

I apologized for coming so unexpectedly, but she quickly said, "Friends don't need previous appointments; it's a compliment to have you come whenever you will."

Sitting on her worn divan, I talked, and she listened, sitting close beside me. With her eyes deep with feeling and understanding, she heard my bitterness and heartache; she shared my tears. Her hand, rough from work and knotted by arthritis, lay gently on mine. I felt her strength, the comfort she gave without saying a word— she who had known so much of sorrow herself.

When the soup was done, she brought it in on a tray, with homemade bread and apricot marmalade, and I thought it was the best lunch I had ever had.

Too quickly the hour passed, and it was time for me to go. I didn't want to, but I knew that I must.

At the door I put an arm around her. "Thank you," I said simply. "I feel so much better now. Could you possibly know how much you have helped me?"

"I don't know why," she said. "I never seem to know what to say, all I can do is listen and try to understand."

Then she raised her eyes upward. "Oh, look!" she exclaimed brightly. "The sky is blue again; tomorrow will be a better day."

Looking up, I saw that she was right. A big patch of blue was pushing the clouds away, and a ray of sunlight gleamed down.

Walking back home with a new perspective, I thought how infinitely wise she was without knowing it.

"I just listen and try to understand," she had said, but oh, the strength she gave in the listening! For to listen is the highest compliment one can give another—to listen and to understand. How rare and precious is a listener.

Her words at parting had given me much to think about—"The sky is blue again." Certainly all things pass away—sorrow, just as cloudy skies, cannot last indefinitely. "Tomorrow will be a better day."

Yes, tomorrow would be a better day because of the selflessness, the charity, of a wonderful friend.

He Works through His Children

PAULINE BAXTER

I was sitting on a crowded bus one morning, en route to my typing class at our local education center, when suddenly I heard a voice within me say, *There is no typing class today; it's the half-term holiday. Get off the bus and go see Sister Benson.*

I looked about in amazement. Slowly I realized that it really was the half-term holiday, and that the bus was fast approaching the stop near Sister Benson's home. The voice had been quiet yet clear and unmistakable, so just before the bus pulled away from the stop, I arose and stepped off.

Feeling rather bewildered, I stood on the street corner in front of a grocery store. "What now?" I wondered. Then the impression came: *Buy some groceries and take them to Sister Benson.*

I peered into my purse. There wasn't much there. Then I looked up and down the road, wondering if I should just catch the next bus home. But the spiritual direction won out: I entered the shop, considered the fact that I was short on money that week and couldn't do the impossible, and decided that I could buy small amounts of the basics—a packet of sugar, a pot of honey, bread, butter, cheese, and one or two other things. These would suffice. "Suffice for what?" I wondered. I paid at the cash desk and once again stood outside on the street corner.

Looking in my purse again, I found I had just enough money to get home on the bus. I also remembered that my own pantry wasn't too well stocked at the moment. "Maybe I'll just go straight home and have these things for myself," I thought. But again the Spirit whispered: *Take those groceries to Sister Benson.* So I set off up the street toward her house.

Sister Benson smiled wearily as she opened the door for me. When I told her that I had brought her a few groceries, her eyes filled with tears. "You shouldn't have done that," she said. But as we talked, I learned that after paying her tithing that week, she had no money left for food. How humble I felt!

The experience taught me once again that the Lord is very much aware of our needs. He is continually working through his children to administer assistance to those in need, and we never know the moment when he may call on us to do just that.

Twinkle Lights

LAUREL CHRISTENSEN

I have always loved Christmas and my festivities for the holiday would start the first of November. It didn't matter how small my college dorm was or how poor my roommates and I were. I had learned how to turn the bleakest basement apartment into a grand festival of Christmas. And my decoration of choice? Twinkle lights. Some people prefer white lights, but I love bold, colored twinkle lights.

After graduating from college, I landed my first real job that was tailor-made for me. Part of my responsibilities included overseeing a popular Christmas production that toured from Thanksgiving to Christmas. I remember thinking that there couldn't be a better job for someone who so devotedly loves Christmas.

Having to give up holiday parties and shopping days seemed to be a small sacrifice at first. In exchange, I was able to travel and go to the theaters and watch all the happy people. I'd hear them say kind things to each other after the show each night. They'd be dressed in their Christmas sweaters and hold hands with the dear friends and family who had joined them for the evening. I knew I was watching memories being made by people who surely appreciated this great musical tradition each Christmas.

But somehow in the midst of this holiday activity, Christmas seemed to stop for me. Or rather, Christmas never started. Consumed with the details of the tour, my favorite holiday didn't ever really make it into my personal life until Christmas Eve. Sometimes I was able to travel home for the holidays. Sometimes I wasn't. It just depended on what day of the week Christmas was, how many shows we had, and when I could use my frequent flyer ticket. Here I was, part of one of the largest Christmas celebrations in the state, but by the time December twenty-fifth rolled around, I didn't have any decorations up, I didn't have any homemade goodies to share, and I didn't feel like hearing one more carol. Somehow my favorite holiday of all holidays got lost.

Then one year I decided something had to change. I knew I would never survive one more Christmas season if I didn't get back to what I had always loved about the holiday.

I mentioned to my friend at work that the first Saturday of November I was going to come in to the office (which wasn't so unusual) not to work (which *was* unusual) but to decorate the office. I told her since I spend far more time at the office during the holidays than I ever do at home, I was going to turn the office into Christmas. I'd bring a tree and decorations and stockings and lights.

Despite my plans, I came to work that Saturday without a tree, decorations, stockings, or lights. I had to work instead and I remember thinking, "After today, it will be too late. This Christmas will be like all the rest."

I turned the corner and walked down the hall. All the lights were off in the building; it was the weekend, all right. It was dark down by my office but I saw a little glimmer of light. As I got closer, I noticed the door was open just a crack. The crack was open just enough to reveal . . . twinkle lights. And not the boring, white, classy ones. These lights were bold. These lights were colorful. These lights were every-thing I loved about Christmas. And someone had brought them to my office for me.

I stood in the doorway looking at all the multicolored lights decorating my office. There I was, a grown-up little girl who had felt a little sad about facing one more Christmas season that would never really start. I had no idea that all I really needed was twinkle lights. And while I didn't hear an angelic choir burst forth holiday hal-lelujahs, I did feel all the warmth that comes when the most simple act of kindness is offered by a friend without obligation, without fanfare, and without request.

The Angel Who Made the Bed

MARK ELLISON

Iet's get a move on, Elder!" I yelled at my lazy missionary companion. Fully dressed in my crisp, new navy blue suit, scriptures in hand, name tag in place, I was ready and eagerly waiting to venture forth from our humble little missionary apartment and preach repentance to the wicked world outside.

My slowpoke companion, however, was still shaving. I paced back and forth in our miniature living room. It was so small that you couldn't pace far. One or two steps in one direction, that was it; then you had to turn. Pace, pace, pace. I waited, then yelled again: "Come on, Elder Raymond!"

"Keep yer shirt on, El-durr!" he hollered back in his Ozark Mountain drawl.

That's my companion, I thought, as I resumed my pacing. My lazy, ball-and-chain, sloth-of-a-missionary companion. Great! I get a burnt-out, trunky, about-to-go-home elder for my first companion in the mission field. I grew red with frustration. Mission rules said we had to be out of our apartment and busy at our missionary labors by nine-thirty each morning. I looked down at my watch. It was ten-forty-seven. I decided it was time to yell again. "It's no wonder we don't have any investigators to teach!"

"Hey!" Elder Raymond's mousy little face, half-covered with shaving cream, appeared in the bathroom doorway. "Put a lid on it, Ellison."

It's kind of funny now to look back on the difficulty I had in getting along with Elder Raymond, but at the time there was nothing funny about it. There I was, on my mission, the experience that was supposed to be the spiritual pinnacle of my life thus far, and I was having these terrible feelings of impatience and anger!

I had never even imagined that my mission would contain the possibility of such contention. But the lifestyle sure was challenging. I was never to leave the presence of my companion. The first thing I'd see in the morning and the last thing I'd see at night was his face. I'd hear his singing, listen to his dumb jokes and the stories about his family, eat his cooking, and see all his weaknesses. He and I seemed totally different: I was raised in the fast-paced subculture of southern California, and he was raised in the hillbilly lands of Missouri. I talked fast, he talked slow.

As the weeks went by, our missionary work seemed to drag. I mean, it was slow—slower than cold molasses trying to drip uphill in January. We couldn't seem to find anyone interested in talking with us. As we encountered disappointment after disappointment I became convinced that it was all Elder Raymond's fault. He was the slow one. I began to miss home, family, girls, my truck, and my guitar. Soon I had developed a truly spectacular case of homesickness, and that, too, was his fault, I felt. I began to hate my companion. And guess what happened to the Spirit in our missionary work? It left. Now, that's no way for a missionary to live.

A terrible dark feeling accompanied this contention. It is the opposite of the love, peace, and joy which accompany the Spirit of the Lord. What could I do?

Elder Richard L. Evans used to say, "Anyone can get along with perfect people, but our task is to get along with imperfect people." I think the Lord understood that we would sometimes have difficulty in doing that. Now, how do you love someone you can't stand, or who can't stand you? I got some ideas when I recalled Jesus' teaching: "Bless them that curse you, do good to them that hate you, and pray for them which despitefully use you, and persecute you" (Matthew 5:44).

One morning, while Elder Raymond was showering, I sat on my bed reading the scriptures. Actually, I was reading a scripture, the same verse, over and over—not because it was especially inspiring, but because I couldn't concentrate. I had to keep thinking, Where was I? and start reading over again. I couldn't concentrate because out of the corner of my eye I could see Elder Raymond's messy bed. I knew it would take him forever to make his bed, get dressed, and be ready to go, and the very thought had me fuming. I yelled toward the bathroom, "Elder, how long are you going to be?" No answer.

Finally, I put my scriptures down, stomped over to my companion's bed, and made it for him, fluffed up the pillow, tucked in the sheets, the works. Then I sat back down on my bed and returned to my reading. I could finally concentrate.

A few minutes later a bathrobe-clad Elder Raymond walked in. He stood in the doorway, looking at the room, perplexed. I pretended not to notice. "Say, El-durr," he drawled, "D'you make mah bed?"

I decided to play innocent. "Why, no, Elder, but it looks really good. Just a sec— I'm almost done with this chapter—and then I'll join you for companion prayer."

"Now, hold on," Elder Raymond muttered, his brow furrowed in thought.

"No, really," I insisted. I was beginning to have fun with this. "It must have been someone else." Then I smiled. "Maybe an angel came down and did it."

That really cracked up Elder Raymond. "An angel, eh? Har, har, har!"

The next morning, as Elder Raymond showered, I quickly made his bed for him again—big fluffy pillow; nice, tight hospital corners, the way my mom had taught me. Then I sat on my bed, read my scriptures, and tried not to laugh. Moments later, in walked my companion. "Say, El-durr, d'you make mah bed again?"

"It wasn't me, Elder, honest."

"Looks like that angel come back again, eh?"

"Yeah, must've been the Angel."

Once again, this struck him as being absolutely hilarious. "Har, har, har, har!"

The Angel struck every morning for a week, and then one morning Elder Raymond said to me, with a half-suppressed grin, "Say. El-durr, why don't yew go shower first today?" I did, and as I came back into the bedroom a few minutes later I noticed that my bed had been made! The pillow fluffed up, the sheets tucked in neatly. Elder Raymond sat on his bed, pretending to be engrossed in the scriptures. I smiled and asked, "Say, El-durr, d'you make mah bed?"

He laughed and said, "Musta been the Angel again!"

From that time on Elder Raymond and I began to do nice things for each other, and we usually blamed them on the mysterious, elusive Angel. I discovered that my companion had a good sense of humor! We began to enjoy each other's company and to sing together as we worked. It lifted our spirits and made our days happier. I no longer hated my companion. I liked him—really, truly, genuinely liked him. And I liked being a missionary again. And guess what happened to the Spirit in our companionship? It came back.

We began to have good experiences talking with people about the gospel. I learned many things from Elder Raymond about how to teach and converse with people. We saw some of our investigators enter the waters of baptism, make covenants with their Father in Heaven, and join the church of his Son, Jesus Christ. We shared many spiritual experiences.

I'll never forget the day when we knocked on the door of a lady who was in terrible pain with a back injury. We taught her about priesthood blessings. Elder Raymond and I laid our hands on her head and blessed her by the power of the Melchizedek Priesthood. The influence of the Spirit was powerful as my good companion boldly declared that this lady's pain would subside immediately. After the blessing, the lady stood with eyes wide and wondering, and quietly spoke: "My pain is gone." Elder Raymond and I testified that we were representatives of the church that held the power and authority of God, and the lady said, "Thank God for young men like you, who go about in the world doing good." And you know what? I began to love my companion. I loved Elder Raymond.

Heart Attack

ARDETH G. KAPP

We've all seen the familiar symbol that communicates the idea of love without any words. We see it on bumper stickers and T-shirts. It is simply the word "I" followed by the shape of a heart and then the word of something someone loves. For example, we read "I love [represented by a heart] snow," or chocolate, or whatever. Hearts signify love in nearly every language.

Early one morning I awakened and walked out on my front porch to look at my flowers. To my surprise I discovered paper hearts stuck all over the front of our house—little hearts, big hearts, red hearts, pink hearts, placed high and low, all over, from one side of the porch to the other. I counted them. There were one hundred in all. On the front door was a very large heart with bold lettering that read, "You're having a heart attack." On the porch was a small basket filled with heart-shaped cookies and a little note with this message: "We love you, Sister Kapp."

I sat down on the porch, in my bathrobe, in my bare feet, and wondered, "Who did this? Why? What's the occasion? What have I done to deserve such attention?" It wasn't my birthday or Valentine's Day, just an ordinary day—that is, until I became invaded with hearts. I can assure you, I did not remove the hearts quickly.

The cookies, yes, but not the hearts. They remained until the setting sun turned the red hearts to pink and the pink to almost white. Neighbors called across the street, "What's the special occasion?" I called back, "Someone loves me," and it felt good just to say that. I didn't discover until several days later that the Laurels from a ward in another stake had come clear across town very early that morning with their hands full of hearts, masking tape, cookies, and love. Love does make the world go around. It certainly made my world go around that day, and each time I think about it.

Eventually I decided to remove the hearts that had created so much attention and happy feelings in our neighborhood. By then they were faded and some slightly torn, but I could not bring myself to throw them away. They lay stacked on a shelf in the garage for several months. One day these faded hearts were called into service once again to perpetuate their message of love. At our family reunion that summer, Uncle Jack and Aunt Nina, the eldest members of the clan, parked their motor home not far from the cabin housing most of the people and all the commotion. In the silence of the night, family members of all ages, with one hundred faded hearts in hand, crept over to the camper and quietly covered the motor home. One large heart on the door said, "You're having a heart attack," and another one said, "We love you."

We all watched excitedly the following morning while Aunt Nina helped Uncle Jack, who had suffered a serious heart attack just months before, step down from the motor home. Then, getting their bearings, they turned around and saw their motor home covered with hearts. "We love you!" everyone shouted. Those hearts had done it again. Tears filled the eyes of many, and we all experienced that tender, wonderful feeling of love.

Tennessee Samaritans

DAVID R. McKINNEY

Most of us, particularly when young, sometimes get ourselves into trouble through ignorance, stupidity, or simple unpreparedness. Often, in these times of distress, the Lord saves us by sending not just one but several good Samaritans to rescue us. One such experience from my college days stands out in my mind.

In 1988, having recently returned from a mission to Japan, I got a summer job as an interpreter with a company based in Nashville, Tennessee. This company provided interpreters to various Japanese auto parts manufacturers in central Tennessee. My main job was to roam the floor of a factory in order to be available to help the Japanese workers communicate as they trained their American counterparts. After hours, we also taught Japanese and English classes for company managers and executives at some of these plants.

One blistering July day, I was assigned to travel about sixty miles north to a small town on the Kentucky border to teach an evening language class. In those days I drove an old green Chevy Impala—my first car—with faded paint, a lot of miles, and no air conditioning. Unfortunately, the temperature was near 105° F. that day.

Cruising north out of Nashville, I couldn't decide which was worse—keeping the windows open and facing a constant blast of hot air, or closing the windows and sweltering in my mobile solar collector. I decided to keep the windows open, but quickly became stickier than a piece of wet wallpaper, pasted by my own sweat to the torn vinyl seats.

As my car climbed a long grade through the rolling hills of north central Tennessee, the heat soon became too much for my old car. The ugly red *TEMP* light began to glow, and I detected the hot, sweet smell of antifreeze. With sweat trickling down my face, I turned on the heater—one of the few right things I knew to do when a car is overheating. Unfortunately, on this day it was not enough to make the difference. I expected that the engine would begin to cool down after I crested the grade, but it did not. A mile or more later it was still overheating, and I decided I had better pull over.

As soon as I came to a stop, steam began wafting out from under the engine compartment. I opened the hood and looked at the engine. A wave of heat poured out. Everything was bubbling and boiling. With a hiss, the radiator overflow bottle bulged and belched hot antifreeze and steam. As cars and trucks whizzed past, I stood there in front of my simmering vehicle wondering what to do. With the engine and the heater still running, I thought the car would gradually cool down and I would be on my way. But as time passed, nothing seemed to change.

That's when I made my critical mistake. I turned off the engine. With the engine off, I thought, the car will surely cool down. Unfortunately, the opposite seemed to happen. I did not understand. The bubbling and boiling only grew louder and more intense. The overflow bottle looked like it might burst.

Suddenly, there was a loud *pop* from underneath the car, followed instantly by a big *whoosh*! I instinctively jumped back, but not before scalding liquid splashed over my left foot, running down into the sides of my low cut slip-on shoes. A giant white plume of steam engulfed the entire front of the car and wafted into the blue summer sky. When the steam cleared, I looked under the car to survey the damage. I was not absolutely certain what had happened, but something had exploded. I hoped it was not too serious. I could see some small wisps of steam still escaping beneath the car. The pain of my foot did not bother me half so much as the realization that I was now stuck on a roadside in the hills of Tennessee, soaked with sweat and hot antifreeze, and unable to make it to my class. To this point I had held in my mind a vague prayer for help—that the Lord would help me in this difficult situation, and help me get to my class. Now my prayers for help became more specific and more urgent.

That's when my first good Samaritan arrived. A red pickup truck slowed as it passed my stalled car, pulled onto the shoulder of the road, then backed up toward me. The driver asked if I needed help, and I explained the situation. He was headed north, and agreed to give me a ride up to the plant where I would be teaching. I would be late, but I felt the need to teach the class, and deal with the car afterward.

I retrieved my lesson materials from my car, and we headed north. In spite of the knots of stress and tension inside me, I enjoyed the ride and the conversation with my rescuer. The fact that his truck had air conditioning didn't hurt, either. He was interested to hear what brought me out to his part of the country, and how I happened to learn Japanese. When we arrived at the plant where I was to teach, I thanked him as sincerely as I could, and wished him well.

Entering the plant office, I found it quiet and empty. There was no receptionist at the front desk. There were no people gathered in the nearby conference room where I normally taught. I was late, I knew, but not *that* late. The vice president of the company was the only one around. I apologized for being late and asked where to go. He said, "Oh, today's class was canceled. Didn't you get the word?" My heart sank. All this trouble, and there never was a class to teach in the first place. But I had a bigger problem on my mind: My car was stalled on the side of the highway twenty miles away and I had no way to get back to it or to home.

The vice president sensed I had troubles and asked what was wrong. I explained the situation. That's when he became my second good Samaritan of the day. He thought for a moment, then said, "If you can wait around here for twenty minutes or so, I can take you back to your car." I gladly accepted and sat down to wait. As I waited, however, I realized that just getting back to my car was not enough. The car needed repairs before it could go anywhere.

When my new rescuer indicated he was ready to go, I mentioned my additional concerns. I felt I could probably fix the car, but needed a new hose to do it. As we left the factory and headed into the nearby town, he offered to take me to an auto parts store to get the parts I would need to fix the car.

The nearby town had perhaps four stoplights. By this time it was after seven o'clock on a summer evening, and nearly everything was closed. There were no big-name auto parts stores, just a couple of mom-and-pop stores on the main street.

We finally found a garage and auto parts store that was still open. I was not absolutely certain what I needed to fix my car, but I told the man on duty what had happened and he said, "Sounds like your lower radiator hose blew." Amazingly, this tiny shop in a small town in rural Tennessee, with very little inventory, just happened to have the right hose for my car. Unfortunately, I didn't have any cash and the shop didn't take credit cards. Again, my rescuer stepped in. Taking money from his own pocket, he paid for the hose, and we were on our way again.

In a few minutes we were back at the site of my poor car. I took a closer look underneath and confirmed that, indeed, the lower radiator hose had burst. With trucks and cars continually blasting past, I crawled under my car and began the repairs. Once I located its ends and the screw heads of the clamps, it took only a few minutes to remove the old hose and replace it with the new one.

The hose was fixed, but it dawned on me that I had nothing to put into the radiator. The old coolant had all drained or evaporated away and the cooling system was entirely empty. Again, good fortune was with me. The vice president who had stood by while I completed the repairs had been to a softball game earlier and still had a cooler in the back of his car with some water in it. In fact, when we looked inside, we discovered that not only did the cooler still contain at least three or four gallons of ice water but it also had two cold soft drinks.

We consumed the cold drinks, then poured the water from the cooler, ice and all, into the radiator. The water filled the radiator about 90 percent full, which was good enough to get me home, or at least to a gas station where I could get more. With the radiator full, I turned the key to start the car, and my old car roared to life.

I thanked my second good Samaritan for his time and kindness, and put my tools back in my car. As I got on the road again, he followed me for a time to be sure that the car was running smoothly, then went his way as I exited to turn around. As I headed back home, I paused to think about what had happened. One man who did not know me at all stopped and went out of his way to help me get to my destination.

Another busy corporate executive, whom I had met only once or twice before, had given generously of his time and also of his money to help me fix my car in a difficult situation. For their trouble, each received only my thanks and a clear conscience. I will never see them again, but I will never forget them either.

As I headed home, nervously watching the *TEMP* light the whole time, I was exhausted, my clothes were filthy, and my foot still burned. But, thanks to two kind people and a series of fortunate coincidences, I was safe and back on the road. I knew these were not mere coincidences, but answers to my prayers. The Lord had arranged events for my good and sent two people to help me. That night, and many times since then, I pondered how remarkable it was that, notwithstanding my youthful foolishness, the Lord was interested enough in my problems to send not just one, but two good Samaritans to rescue me.

"Love, Your Visiting Teachers"

MELINDA R. SUTTNER

early in our marriage, my husband, David, and I bought an old "fixer-upper" house in Clarksville, Tennessee. We gutted the insides, ripped up some of the floors, replaced the wiring and plumbing, and added on to make a duplex. It was a major undertaking! And we stayed in the house the whole time.

Needless to say, we lived in a veritable construction site. At night before falling into bed, I'd rake the sawdust, sheetrock, chips of wood, and other debris from the sheets. I used a corn scoop, a type of large shovel, instead of a broom to clean the floors. Lumber and sheets of plywood were stacked in the living room. Batts of insulation, rolls of wallpaper, cans of paint, boxes of nails, and ladders, tools, and sawhorses decorated other rooms.

During the remodeling, I was pregnant with our second daughter, Caci. On a weekend two weeks before my due date, we stained the floors and painted the addition. Monday morning, the baby started coming. We rushed to the hospital, leaving behind a house with no heating system, no windows in the living room, and no place for an infant to sleep.

Mama and Daddy came to the hospital that afternoon, driving the sixty-five miles from their backwoods farm near Crofton, Kentucky. I was apprehensive about Mama coming. She and I hadn't been on good terms since I joined the Church in 1976. But she knew I needed help, with a new baby and the house all torn apart.

Before returning home, Mama stopped by the construction site. Overwhelmed—and a little dismayed at the living conditions her new grandchild would be brought into—she made plans to clean the house the next afternoon before I came home from the hospital.

Mama came as planned, clad in work clothes, with shovel, rake, and bucket in hand. To her surprise, the construction site was spotless. Lumber, plywood, wallpaper, paint, and tools were all neatly stacked in one room. Clean sheets were on the bed. A bassinet with a new mattress and new sheets waited for Caci. The dirty laundry was missing. A fast-food lunch for David was in the refrigerator. And a wrapped package of baby clothes and a large bag of disposable diapers sat near the front door. The card attached read, "Congratulations! Love, your visiting teachers, Carol and Barbara."

I hardly knew these sisters—they had been called to be my visiting teachers only the month before. But when I came home from the hospital the next day, Carol brought the freshly washed laundry. Barbara brought supper—roast hen and dressing, vegetables, salad, homemade rolls, and dessert. Although it was only October, we felt as if Thanksgiving had arrived.

But something else had happened, too.

Mama had taken the missionary discussions while I was on my mission. She had even read the four Standard Works and *Teachings of the Prophet Joseph Smith*. But her heart did not begin to soften until she saw the gospel in action.

Mama and I had a long talk later that week. We hugged each other for the first time in years. Tears fell long into the night, and we felt a closeness as mother and daughter again.

We currently live in the West, and I look forward to Mama's calls and letters. We wouldn't have traveled back to Kentucky with our three daughters last summer—four thousand miles round-trip—if it hadn't been for Carol and Barbara, my visiting teachers of long ago. They had come to clean a house and cook a meal. But they had no way of knowing that they were mending hearts and healing wounds and putting a home back together again.

He Still Had His Old Ones

MICHAELENE P. GRASSLI

It was a bitter cold winter in southeast Idaho, and eleven-year-old Kelly had barely had time to arrive at school when he telephoned his mother.

"Mom, could you bring my old coat to school, please?" he asked.

"Why, Kelly?"

"Because I gave my new one away."

His mother tried to remain calm. "You *what?*"

"Mom, one of the Indian boys from the reservation came this morning with no coat on, and, Mom, his ears were frostbitten, and he was crying." The temperatures had been below zero. "Mom, he stood and waited for the bus for half an hour. I gave him my hat and my gloves too. I hope you don't mind. I knew I still had my old ones."

A Chance to Dance

SHANE BARKER

as a teacher I was supervising a school dance when I saw Teresa, a girl from one of my classes. She was standing off to the side, all by herself. She wasn't an attractive girl, and she wasn't very popular. I knew that she wasn't going to dance much.

But I happened to know that she liked a boy named Mike. (She had his name written all over her folders.)

It also happened that Mike was a friend of mine, so I went up to him and said, "How'd you like to do me a favor?"

"Sure."

"There's a girl I'd like you to dance with. Would you ask her?"

My respect for Mike went up 100 percent. He didn't ask who she was; he simply said, "Sure."

I pointed her out. And my admiration for him went up another 100 percent. He didn't pull a face. And he didn't say, "Boy, you're gonna owe me big for this one." Instead, he just nodded.

"Okay," he said. "Do you want me to ask her right now?"

I shook my head. "No. Just sometime. I just think it would be cool if she got a chance to dance tonight."

"Okay," he said again. "I'll do it."

He did, too. I saw them as they walked onto the dance floor, and she was glowing.

But the classy thing about Mike was that he asked her *twice more*.

Mike lifted a life that night. With no thought for himself—and without worrying what anyone would think—he blessed Teresa's life.

"Singing Was in My Heart"

MARY JOHANSEN

e ven as a child I loved to sing. I would go into my room after church on Sunday and draw pictures and sing and sing, until my mother came to the door to say, "Mary, please don't sing so loud in there. It's not that we don't like to know you are happy, honey, but you know you just can't carry a tune."

Singing was in my heart, though, and I would go up into the woods behind our house and run through the woods singing all the songs I wanted to: Sad songs that broke my heart and I'd cry, and happy songs that made me feel so good I'd laugh out loud.

When I married and had my first child, I would sit and sing the loveliest songs to him. Songs I made up from my heart to tell him how much I loved him—how special he was to me. And he would smile and cuddle closer to me and fall asleep in my arms as I sang my songs of joy.

Each child, then, received his or her own special song, made up just for that child, telling of my feelings and love for him. I sang only when there was no one around, for my husband agreed with my mother: "I'm sorry, honey, but you sound just awful when you sing."

The children didn't seem to mind my off-tune voice at all. In fact, we sang wonderful play songs together, laughing and playing and enjoying the sound of our voices. Many happy hours were spent sitting, marching, walking, and playing games with singsong instructions.

After having four wonderful children, I received my greatest joy—twin boys! What a blessing. How wonderful it was to sit and hold them in my arms for hours, singing of my love for them while they cuddled close to me and then fell asleep.

Because everyone had always told me that my singing voice left much to be desired, I hesitated to sing for anyone except the babies. In church, even though I knew the Lord loved to hear us sing, my "noise unto the Lord" was a very soft noise. And at home I always made sure the house was empty before I picked up my hymnbook to sing my favorites.

One evening after the children had all gone to bed and my husband had duty at the Navy base, I picked up my hymnbook and began to sing "How Gentle God's Commands." I sang and felt the great love of our Heavenly Father who loves us so much even though we disregard his gentle commands.

"O My Father," I sang, aching to go back to his home where I could be with him again.

"The Lord Is My Light"—my favorite—I sang with all the love I felt in my heart for the guidance he had given me in my life.

Finishing my singing, I put my head in my arms and poured out my heart to my Heavenly Father, thanking him for the love he had for us, and for the great feeling of peace that came to me when I could sit and sing to him and talk to him, escaping from this mortal world for even a few minutes.

Then I turned out the lights and went upstairs to my room. I noticed a sheet of paper on the dresser that hadn't been there before. I picked it up, and tears came to my eyes as I read:

Mom

I don't care what any one says about your singing voice. But I think it was so butiful the way you sang them songs. I was crying in my bed wile I was lisenning to you sing, and I love you very much.

love from your
daughter Barbara.

I found her with tears in her eyes in her bed. "Oh, Barbie," I said, "you are the only person who has ever told me she likes my singing. Thank you, honey." She hugged me back and sobbed, "Mommie, I just couldn't let it go. I had to get out of bed and write that note to you. I was crying listening to your beautiful singing."

I thought later that if our Heavenly Father loves my voice so much he inspires my daughter to write me a lovely note and share her feelings with me, he must love to hear us sing more than I realize.

The next Sunday when we sang the opening song, I sang out just as loud as the rest of the people did. My Heavenly Father liked my voice, and that was all that mattered to me!

The Last Room

J A M I E   G R O S S

It was October of 1997 and I was about to move from Utah to Minnesota with my wife, KyLee, and our baby daughter, Mykenze. While we had many adventures on our trip—some of them good, some of them not so good—one event stands out in my mind as an example of selflessness and charity.

We had packed and were planning to leave on Saturday morning. But by Friday afternoon, the weatherman was predicting a bad winter storm headed our way. My wife and I decided to leave immediately to try to get ahead of the storm.

As we left Utah the snow started falling, but the roads were not bad yet so we kept driving. We seemed to be ahead of the storm as we pulled into Evanston, Wyoming, around five o'clock that night.

My wife and I discussed whether we should stay in Evanston for the night or continue on. The roads were getting worse, icy and slick, and I was having a hard time keeping our heavy moving truck under control, but we both agreed that we should keep moving. We got back on the road but after traveling about another fifty miles we discovered how wrong we were. While we were stopped in Evanston the storm had had a chance to catch up.

It was not long before the weather was so bad that we couldn't see more than twenty feet in front of us. When you are traveling at twenty miles an hour, freeway exits do not come along very often. We finally spotted an exit that promised a little hotel in the town. We drove down the off-ramp and stopped. None of the roads were plowed and we couldn't see the town. Rather than risk getting stuck on the small roads, we got back on the freeway.

We traveled for about three more hours before we came upon signs for another hotel. The weather had gotten worse, if such a thing was possible, and the freeway exit was lined with eighteen-wheel trucks parked off to the side. We pulled off the freeway and inched into the hotel parking lot, which was already packed with cars and big rigs.

We headed toward the hotel to see if we could get a room. As we approached the door a trucker stopped us and told us there were no rooms left but that his truck had a sleeper cab on it and he would be happy to let us stay there. I did not feel very good about that idea. Maybe I was being paranoid, but it felt too much like a scene out of a horror movie for me. I thanked him, but told him that we were going to check on the rooms anyway. So with four-month-old Mykenze wrapped inside my jacket, we went to the front desk. As the trucker had warned, the hotel was sold out.

With no choice left to us, we decided to sleep in our truck. At least there was a gas station next to the hotel so we did not need to worry about running out of gas. Just as we were settling in for the night, there was a knock on the window of our truck. Startled, I slowly rolled down the window. It was the man from the front desk. He said, "One of the truckers that was in the lobby had just booked the last room, but he said he wanted your family to have it." KyLee and I did not know what to say other than thank you.

We got into the hotel room and knelt at the bedside and gave thanks to our Heavenly Father for watching out for us on our trip. And this time we added a special, heartfelt thank you for the wonderful person who was willing to give up his bed on a cold, snowy night for us.

Bearing One Another's Burdens

JILL B. BRADY

Our ward campout was scheduled for Friday and Saturday, August 23 and 24, exactly when my husband, Scott, and I needed to be away from Phoenix to take two of our children to college out of state. Because Jordan, our thirteen-year-old son, had already started school and did not want to miss the campout, we left him in the care of a family in our ward.

During the last few hours of the campout, Jordan and his friend Robbie decided to ride another friend's four-wheeler one more time. They didn't tell anyone they were leaving and headed out along the dirt road leading away from camp. They were having a great time but traveling too fast to negotiate a curve in the rocky road. They flew off the road and struck a tree. The driver of a pickup truck going in the opposite direction saw the accident happen. He turned around and went back to see if they were all right. That was the first of numberless good deeds of love and service for Jordan, Robbie, and their families.

The man who stopped was a retired firefighter. He stayed with the seriously injured boys until the paramedics arrived. Cell phones did not work in the area, but someone else who had stopped to help had a radio and called for help. Paramedics at nearby Mormon Lake overheard the radio transmission and set off for the accident site even before they were notified from the dispatch unit. They arrived within minutes.

Ward members at the campout quickly gathered and said a prayer. Priesthood holders went to the accident site, stayed with the boys, and gave blessings to both of them, which was a great comfort to all concerned.

The paramedics determined that both boys needed to be life-flighted to the nearest hospital. Miraculously, three helicopters were already in the air on a practice mission. They landed in a large meadow near the accident site only minutes after being notified. The boys were flown to a hospital in Flagstaff, Arizona.

His pelvis fractured in five places and his arm broken, Robbie stayed in the hospital in Flagstaff. A bishop in the area who managed a motel provided the family with a suite for as long as they needed it. Individuals from three different wards took meals to the family for nearly four weeks. None of these people had known Robbie or his family before the accident. Members of our own ward, who lived two hours distant from Flagstaff, rotated almost daily to lend companionship and support to Robbie and his family.

Jordan, who had suffered multiple skull fractures, was life-flighted from Flagstaff to a hospital in Phoenix. Meanwhile, his father and I had been told of the accident. We flew home immediately, arriving at the hospital just in time to sign medical forms and kiss our son before he was taken into surgery. Family members and friends waited with us through the night. Blessings of comfort were given, food was brought, and many prayers were offered during those crucial hours.

After the surgery, early Sunday morning, the doctors suggested that all of our children should join us at the hospital as soon as possible. Even though the surgery had slowed the dangerous swelling of Jordan's brain, the doctors were not optimistic about his survival. We quickly contacted ward members by phone and by e-mail, asking them to fast with us that day. Plane tickets were secured so that our children who were in Utah could fly home; reimbursement to the donors was declined.

We drew strength from the fasting, prayers, and other good deeds of friends, family, and even strangers as Jordan lay unconscious, seemingly close to death. His condition gradually began to improve. While he was in the hospital, a meal was provided for us each day—including plates, utensils, and napkins. Our children were given rides to school, seminary, and work every day, and were taken to the hospital to be with us in the evening. Our van, which had broken down while we were in Utah, was repaired and then driven back to Arizona for us; again, reimbursement was declined. Free baby-sitting was provided for our two-year-old, Anna, who stayed with friends during the day until twelve-year-old Erica and sixteen-year-old Kristina went to the hospital in the evening. All three girls and our dinner arrived together—every night for eight weeks.

Grandma Brady called each evening and each morning wrote e-mails to extended family and friends about Jordan's progress. A friend came each morning to rub Jordan's legs, give him a pep talk, and encourage us. He even returned in the evenings to twist balloons to brighten the room.

Jordan's walls were soon covered with get-well cards from friends far and near, family, classmates at school, and teachers. A CD player appeared with music and tapes for Jordan to listen to. Balloons galore decorated his room. Gifts for Anna, Erica, and Kristina also appeared. A handmade heart with quotations for each day hung on Jordan's wall. Many stuffed animals were brought to his room. We used some of them for pillows.

Hugs from countless visitors brought spiritual strength that was desperately needed. Songs were sung and prayers were offered around Jordan's bed by friends and family.

The days came and went. Still Jordan was unconscious. The surgery to reconstruct his face was successful, and our hope for his recovery grew. Bishopric members and friends visited several times and played card games in the waiting room with our children. Someone gave us tickets to a baseball game so that we could have a break from our constant attendance at the hospital. Someone else gave us an anonymous gift of a suite for a Suns basketball game, to be used when Jordan was doing better.

Flowers were brought to our home to brighten our days there and to celebrate stages of Jordan's progress. The Young Women of a neighboring ward made a quilt for Jordan and another one for Erica, with each individual quilting a square. Other blankets were made with love and shared. Pictures of Christ were given to us to put on the wall in Jordan's room. We completely redecorated his hospital room. At the end of our eight-week stay, the doctors were sure it would take a week just to move out.

A camcorder was lent to us to record Jordan's progress. Friends would come and sit and talk with Jordan while we both needed to be gone. Pep talks in English and Spanish were whispered into Jordan's ears while he was unconscious. We had a sign-in book where all of Jordan's visitors wrote their names. They had to sign each time they visited. One sister came almost every day for two weeks and read the visitors' recorded thoughts to Jordan while he was still in a coma. Another sister visited every day just to be there if she was needed; she brought water, treats, games—whatever might be needed.

Four weeks after the accident, Jordan took his first steps, with the considerable support of his physical therapists. They and his occupational and speech therapists worked patiently with him to help him regain lost skills. Our ward members continued to fast whenever requested, and family and friends offered prayers continually. Generous gifts of time and money and service poured in. Fund-raising activities included a "Water for Jordan" week, in which businesses in the town in Oregon where Jordan was born sold bottled water and donated the proceeds to help our son. The local youth sponsored a car wash. Other family members and friends contributed to our family money that they had earned from other kinds of projects especially designed to help Jordan.

Six weeks after the accident, Jordan was able to attend church. The bishopric, Young Men's presidency, deacons quorum members, and other men in the ward wore bow ties that day in his honor. That day, too, Jordan passed the sacrament for the first time since the accident. His elder brother, Mitchell, shadowed him to assist if necessary.

Two weeks later, Jordan came home from the hospital to stay. The long process of his miraculous recovery continues, aided by the thoughtful actions of many, many people who continue to give of their time and means and service.

Post Office Stamps

MARY ELLEN EDMUNDS

i had an unforgettable experience a few years ago on a hot August evening. I stopped at the post office to get my mail. It's always after hours when I go there, so usually there's no one around. But that evening as I walked in I noticed a man standing at the automatic stamp dispenser looking frustrated. He looked as if he might have come from Mexico; many come from there to help us harvest our crops.

This man was trying to get the stamp machine to take his money and give him some stamps but was apparently having problems. I took all of this in as I turned and walked to my box. A strong, deep feeling came into my heart that I wanted to help the man get his stamps. And I had a distinct impression: "This is compassion you're feeling."

I got my mail, sorted it, and then walked over to the man. "Isn't it working, sir?" "No," he replied, looking at me helplessly. I had never used one of those machines, but I wanted so much to help that I said, "Let me try." I took his extremely worn five-dollar bill and tried to get the machine to take it. I tried several times. All kinds of approaches. It wouldn't work.

I handed the bill back to the man and mumbled something like, "It won't work." He looked back at me as if to say, "That's what I said." I said, "Hold on a sec." He obviously had no idea what I meant. I went to my car (thinking he probably thought I had left and wouldn't be back) and returned with my purse. I took out my three newest one-dollar bills and approached the machine.

The man was watching with what seemed to be a whole lot of curiosity. I put a dollar bill in, and the machine took it. I shouted, "Yippee!" The machine took the other two one-dollar bills, too, and with a sense of accomplishment and joy I said, "Sir! It's working!" We got a book of stamps and a dime for change. That was my first experience with such a machine, and I wanted the man to be as excited as I was.

This was happiness. I handed the book and the dime to the man and said, "Sir, we got it! Here you go!" He started shaking his head no. I said, "Yes—these are yours." He backed away a bit saying, "No, no—you don't do this . . ." I said, "Yes, I do—I just did! These are your stamps."

He wouldn't take them. I didn't know what to do. Then I got an idea. I said the first thing that came into my mind on that very hot August day: "Merry Christmas, sir!" He had to smile. He couldn't help it. He took the stamps and the dime.

Then he looked at his worn five-dollar bill, and I sensed it was all he had. He asked hesitantly, with an accent, "How much I owe you?" I said, "Nothing. *Nada.*" He seemed confused. "No," he said and tried to give the stamps back to me. I wouldn't take them, but I didn't want him to feel bad. So I said, "Sir, you would do the same for me." He kind of smiled at that and nodded yes, he would. I told him I knew that.

I walked out of the post office on Cloud Ten. I felt so wonderful. It hit me: three minutes, three bucks—cheap! I treasured that genuine feeling of joy and shouted happily all the rest of the way home.

"Unto One of the Least of These"

SUSAN FARR-FAHNCKE

h e was kind of scary. He sat there on the grass with his cardboard sign and his dog (actually his dog was adorable). Tattoos ran up and down both arms and even reached his neck. The sign proclaimed him to be "stuck and hungry" and asked for help.

A sucker for anyone needing help, I pulled the van over and in my rearview mirror contemplated this man, tattoos and all. He was youngish, maybe forty. He wore a bandanna tied over his head, biker-pirate style. Anyone could see that he was dirty and had a scraggly beard. But if you looked closer, you could see that he had neatly tucked in his black T-shirt and that his things were in a small, tidy bundle. Nobody was stopping for him. I could see the other drivers take one look and immediately focus on something else—anything else.

It was so hot out. I could see in the man's very blue eyes how dejected and tired and worn out he felt. The sweat was trickling down his face. As I sat with the air conditioning blowing, a scripture suddenly popped into my head: "Inasmuch as ye have done it unto one of the least of these my brethren, ye have done it unto me" (Matthew 25:40).

I reached down into my purse and extracted a ten-dollar bill. My twelve-year-old son, Nick, knew right away what I was doing. "Can I take it to him, Mom?"

"Be careful, honey," I warned, and handed him the money. I watched in the mirror as he rushed over to the man and with a shy smile gave him the bill. I saw the man, startled, stand and take the money, putting it into his back pocket. Good, I thought to myself. Now he will at least have a hot meal tonight. I felt satisfied, proud of myself. I had made a sacrifice and now I could go on with my errands.

When Nick got back into the car, however, he looked at me with sad, pleading eyes. "Mom, his dog looks so hot and the man is really nice." I knew I had to do more.

"Go back and tell him to stay there, that we will be back in fifteen minutes," I told Nick. He bounded out of the car and ran to tell the tattooed stranger.

We then drove to the nearest store and chose our gifts carefully. "It can't be too heavy," I explained to the children. "He has to be able to carry it around with him." We finally settled on our purchases: a bag of "Ol' Roy" (I hoped it was good—it looked good enough for me to eat! How do they make dog food look that way?), a flavored chew toy shaped like a bone, a water dish, bacon-flavored snacks (for the dog), two bottles of water (one for the dog, one for Mr. Tattoos), and some people snacks for the man.

We rushed back to the spot where we had left him, and there he was, still waiting. And still nobody else was stopping for him. With hands shaking, I grabbed our bags and climbed out of the car, all four of my children following me, each carrying gifts. As we walked up to him I had a fleeting moment of fear and hoped he wasn't a serial killer.

I looked into his eyes and saw something that startled me and made me ashamed of my judgment. I saw tears. He was fighting like a little boy to hold back his tears. How long had it been since someone had showed this man kindness? I told him I hoped it wasn't too heavy for him to carry and showed him what we had brought. He stood there like a child at Christmas, and I felt that my small contributions were so inadequate. When I took out the water dish, he snatched it out of my hands as if it were solid gold and told me he had had no way to give water to his dog. He gingerly set it down, filled it with the bottled water we brought, and stood up to look directly into my eyes. His were so blue, so intense. My own filled with tears as he said, "Ma'am, I don't know what to say." He then put both hands on his bandanna-clad head and just started to cry. This man—this "scary" man—was so gentle, so sweet, so humble.

I smiled through my tears and said, "Don't say anything." Then I noticed the tattoo on his neck. It said: "Mama tried."

As we all piled into the van and drove away, he was on his knees, arms around his dog, kissing the animal's nose and smiling. I waved cheerfully and then fully broke down into tears. I had so much. My worries seemed so trivial and petty now. I had a home, a loving husband, four beautiful children. I had a bed. I wondered where he would sleep that night.

My stepdaughter, Brandie, turned to me and said in the sweetest little-girl voice, "I feel so good!"

Although it seemed that we had helped him, the man with the tattoos had really given us a gift that we would never forget. He had taught us that no matter what we look like on the outside, each of us is a child of God inside, deserving kindness, compassion, and acceptance. He opened my heart.

Tonight and every night I pray for the gentle man with the tattoos and his dog. And I hope that God will send more people like him into my life to remind me of what's really important.

A LifeSaver in the Grand Canyon

JIM AND CAROL GEIL

*W*e . . . are . . . climb . . . ing . . . Ja . . . cob's . . . lad . . . der, . . . we . . . are . . . climb . . . ing . . . Ja . . . cob's . . . lad . . . der—I take a step with each syllable, then repeat. I don't remember the rest of the song. It doesn't matter. Nothing matters but taking the next step and getting my family up this endless trail and out of the Grand Canyon.

"Look, Matty and Mark. This part of the trail is called Jacob's Ladder. This is a song about it."

"Ladder, what ladder?" Matty turns in the carrier on my back, almost throws me off balance. Mark plods silently by my side, eyes on the ground. I'm worried the most about him. This is too hard a trek for a five year old.

"This isn't a real ladder, but all of these turns make it look like one." Switchbacks spiral upward through the dry gray-yellow limestone. I see no end to them.

We round a bend and reach my wife and older sons, leaning against their backpacks. "What took you so long? Let's go." Twelve-year-old Tim gets up and pulls on his pack.

"No, I still want to rest," nine-year-old Abe says as he slumps against his pack.

Mark collapses next to Abe and speaks for the first time since leaving Indian Gardens. "I can't walk any more."

"Here's some water. It's warm, like we are." My wife holds the half-full bottle for Mark to take a drink, then offers it to Matty, and finally to me. "We'll get more water at the Three Mile House."

If we ever reach it. Suddenly I shiver in the heat.

Other hikers pass us. A gray-haired man with a day pack strides briskly up the trail. He pauses, reaches into the pocket of his shorts and hands me two packages of peppermint LifeSavers. "Perhaps these will help."

I pass the first package around. Mark takes a candy, places it on the tip of his tongue, then swirls it around in his mouth. He gets up and takes a step forward. He looks up at the gray-yellow switchbacks and the red wall beyond. "This does look like a ladder, Daddy. To get us to the top."

We are climbing Jacob's ladder, we are climbing Jacob's ladder, we are climbing Jacob's ladder—stairway to the stars.

From the Ward, with Love

JANET FARLEY RICHARDSON

i remember in early 1982 saying, "Gee, nothing exciting ever happens to us."
Things were going rather well for our family; we had no financial problems, and
we felt secure and happy.

But things soon changed. In April, my husband, Chad, had to have surgery on
an old knee injury. Shortly after his surgery, he was involved in a motorcycle accident in which he again injured his knee, as well as his back.

During this time, several other members of our family also suffered injuries. To
make matters worse, my husband found out that his job was being terminated on
November 13. On November 6 he broke his wrist and had to have another operation,
so he didn't get to work his final week.

The day after our bishop learned of our pending unemployment, my visiting
teacher, Carol, stopped by to see what we needed. Right then, all I needed was a
shoulder to cry on. She listened to me while months of pent-up emotions came out.

Because of Chad's recent surgery, he was not eligible for unemployment benefits. We weren't too worried about that; we had our food storage and felt we could survive. But Christmas was coming, and we were not looking forward to it. We didn't

know when Chad would be able to return to work, and we didn't want to spend a lot of money on gifts.

One evening Carol called to ask if we would come to her house for a family home evening on December 20. We accepted the invitation. Each time I saw her after that, I asked if we could bring anything for the program, but she assured me that it was all arranged.

On Sunday evening, December 19, she came to our house with invitations for everyone. They read:

Out of the 1,437 families in this area, yours has been selected as the winner in the fabulous "This Is Your Night Sweepstakes." Congratulations! You have won:

1. Dependable Limousine Service for the evening's affairs
2. Dinner at VC's and the Supper Club by candlelight
3. Delightful entertainment at Barney's
4. Delivery back home in time for family prayer and scripture study

We live in a rural area of New Mexico where there isn't any limousine service. We had never heard of VC's, the Supper Club, or Barney's. We could hardly wait until Monday night to see what Carol was planning.

The next evening at 5:30, a station wagon belonging to one of the families in our ward arrived, with a sign reading "Dependable Limousine Service" on the side. Inside were one of my husband's seminary students and my visiting teacher's son. Dressed as chauffeurs, with suits, hats, and gloves, they came to our door and asked for the "Richardson party."

We got into the car and were driven to Carol's house, the "Supper Club." Here the children got out and were treated to a spaghetti dinner by candlelight. Chad and I were driven to "VC's," Vi and Charles Maxwell's house. By my plate was a lovely corsage Vi had made of Christmas flowers. We ate a steak dinner they had prepared, feeling like royalty all the while.

As soon as we finished our dinner, the "chauffeurs" appeared at the door. They had already picked up the children. Our next stop was "Barney's," which turned out to be the home of Tom Murray, our home teacher. (Barney is the Murrays' dog.) At the Murrays' we were given our choice of five video movies to watch. Hot popcorn was waiting—just like at the movies.

Chad and I were so grateful. We couldn't believe how much these people had prepared for this night while keeping it all a secret from us! After the movie we had refreshments of marshmallow treats and root beer. We were then driven home in the "limousine."

My sister and her family were scheduled to arrive from Texas sometime that night to spend the Christmas holidays with us. They were already there when we arrived at home.

On the table in the dining room was a huge box of supplies for Christmas baking—including flour, sugar, chocolate chips, and milk. I asked my sister if she had brought it. She said, "No, we found it by your door and brought it in."

Then the doorbell rang. It was another family in our ward, loaded with gifts and candy—a tied quilt for Chad and me, and two gifts for each of the children. The joy on my children's faces was so touching; it made me cry.

My sister, who is not a member of the Church, could not believe all that was taking place. She said, "This is unheard-of where I live. No one does anything like this in our church."

When I called Carol on the telephone to thank her for all the planning she had done to make the evening one we would never forget, she wouldn't tell me who gave all the food and gifts. It was "just friends who wanted to help and be a part of your Christmas," she said.

The giving did not stop. Throughout the Christmas holidays, others came by with special gifts for our family. Truly, this was love unfeigned—the kind of love that Christmas is all about.

"It's a Miracle"

TOM HEWITSON

i was born and raised in Salt Lake City, Utah, and despite the fact that both my mom and dad came from very strong Mormon pioneer roots, church activity became unimportant somewhere along the line. Dad was a truck driver and on the road most of the time. Mom worked as a mortgage loan officer by day and ran a pretty tight ship at home. Life was good, but something was missing.

It was the winter of 1967 and I was seven years old. I had been outside playing in the fresh mounds of snow with my friends when Mom called us in for dinner. I remember it was her delicious spaghetti and my older brother and sister knew that afterward the three of us would be washing and drying the dishes. It was a time of innocence and great imagination. My brother and I were choreographing a slow-motion battle scene with butter knives when I accidentally leaned against the cord of the boiling hot coffee percolator. In an instant, the fun turned to extreme panic as the percolator dumped coffee all over the right side of my head and right shoulder. Mom heard me scream and rushed into the kitchen. She was quick to react, pulling off my shirt and some skin and hair with it. Mom had my sister call a friend who lived a few blocks away, and in an instant the three of us were on our way to the hospital.

The emergency physician told Mom that I had second- and third-degree burns and would need skin grafts and plastic surgery for the next year. I had a restless night, and the gauze and bandages wrapped around my head and shoulder were uncomfortable. I cried a lot from the pain, but tried to be brave. The next day my dad came home from the road. It was one of the few times I ever saw him cry. The day seemed to last forever, with concerned family and a few neighbors visiting into the evening. Just when it seemed to calm down, the doorbell rang.

A silver-haired grandpa stood at the door. He was dressed in a red plaid flannel shirt and jeans, carrying a plate of sugar cookies. Mother welcomed him in. As he looked down at me his glasses slipped toward the end of his nose, and he said, "Hi, Tommy, I'm Vern Jackman." He smelled of Old Spice aftershave and I remember how gentle his voice was. He sat the cookies down on the nightstand next to me and patted my hand while he visited with Mom and Dad for a short while. He asked if it would be okay to leave with a word of prayer and asked Dad to pray but he declined. So Vern said a lovely prayer and blessed our home.

As soon as he said "amen" he asked Mom and Dad if he could give me a priesthood blessing. I had never heard of such a thing, but my parents were happy to accept the offer. He took out his car keys, and connected to them was a small cylinder of consecrated oil. He anointed the crown of my head with oil that had been "consecrated and dedicated for the blessing and healing of the sick and afflicted." The words he spoke were soothing to all of us. There was an indescribable warmth that came over me, and a sense of peace filled our home.

In the days to come, Vern checked up on me quite often. He would occasionally bring another silver-haired grandpa and they would visit and teach our family about the Church. I enjoyed the good feeling that was in our home after they left and loved the lingering scent of Old Spice aftershave.

A few months passed, and thanks to Mom and my first grade teacher, I was able to get my schoolwork completed at home. Christmastime passed and then the New Year. The daily changing of bandages became routine. Then in January of 1968, my doctor made an unforgettable announcement.

"No skin grafts or plastic surgery necessary," said the doctor. "It's a miracle."

I was completely healed.

How those words "it's a miracle" vividly sing in my mind as I reflect back on that winter of my young life. How they changed the lives of my mom and dad and brother and sister. Through the faith of a silver-haired grandpa, his service and friendship, and his unconditional love for his neighbors, our lives were so dearly touched.

I remember looking out among the congregation some years later during my missionary farewell. There, sitting on the front row, was Vern Jackman. His glasses had slipped down toward the end of his nose and he was grinning from ear to ear when he winked at me.

Vern has since passed on to the next wonderful adventure that awaits us all. But the blessings he helped bring into our family still continue. His legacy reminds me of how I want to live my life. And in memory and as a reminder, I still wear Old Spice aftershave.

"There Is Room in Our Inn"

LAPREAL WIGHT

if you keep my commandments . . ." And she had kept his commandments. This thought came to me suddenly and impressively the day Mary Hurren Wight walked into her kitchen with the sick child in her arms. It was not her child, for she was seventy years of age; nor was it the child of her relatives. It was the sick child of total strangers, people bogged down with trouble and a broken car, camped under the locust tree at the edge of the lane.

Mary's children rose up in protective alarm.

"Mother! You might be exposing the whole family to something terrible," they remonstrated. "You don't know what the child has. It could have anything!"

"It is not a question of what it has or could have," she answered firmly. "The child is sick. A little baby cannot be sick inside a wretched car—with Mormon homes about it. Every house has a door. Doors were made to let people in. And when has my door ever been shut?"

"We know," they continued. "But there is so much one could do without bringing the child home."

"That's just it," triumphantly replied their mother. "Home—why, this innocent young one has no home! We have a warm, happy one—and there is room at our inn. Besides, in a way these people are strangely close to us, camped as they are under our locust tree. Literally, they are our neighbors."

Linked by common understanding of their mother's purpose, which had always seemed clear and fixed when she was serving her fellowmen, the girls decided their mother had made the right decision. It may have been, also, that they saw the sick child's face, and with one accord they agreed they should call a doctor.

"Yes, immediately," said Mary, "although there is not much a body can do at this stage. The little soul is so near to making its last earthly flight. I doubt that even a doctor can help." Then she added, slowly, "I think you had better put a bite to eat on the table. The child's mother will be here. She's hungry. Her husband is hungry also. They have been worried, those two. I guess they never thought of food. At least they did not have any. I asked them. Set the table for two."

Mary Hurren Wight was my grandmother, and I never came in close contact with her that I did not realize that I was in the presence of a good woman. But I think I had never known until the following two days just how much strength there is in a beautiful soul like hers. For in spite of everything one could do, there was a moment when the baby smiled up at us, gratefully, it seemed, for its warm, clean bed in Mary's kitchen; then, with a little sigh of such sweet content, it closed its eyes peacefully, and its soul winged homeward.

Later, husband and wife approached Mary, their hands clasped together, his arm laid consolingly about his partner's shoulder. There was a mystified horror in his eyes, and his speech was awkward and hesitant in its despair.

"Could we . . . would we be able to . . . well, his mother and I would like a little sermon preached before we bury him. Would it cost too much?"

"Not a penny," Mary promised them. "My church does not take money for preaching."

As she continued to explain to them our beliefs, I saw the fear leave their faces, and in its place adoration for this aged woman lit up their countenances, and they appeared gallant in their sorrow. I felt that throughout their years no one had stopped to be kind to them before. And they were the type that needed kindness. They had probably needed it many times along their way. If someone had lent a hand, they might never have had to face the sorrow that was theirs to bear at that moment.

When I heard the simple voices of neighbors ring out in song—a funeral hymn—in Mary's front parlor, and saw the humble, grateful tears in the eyes of the still bewildered parents as they looked upon the little pine box, made by other neighbors' hands; when I smelled the faint odor of Mary's garden flowers adding color to the casket, making it appear beautiful and fragrant; when I heard the bishop speak of life eternal, I was proud of my grandmother, for I realized she had brought this good moment about. I was a witness to the keeping of the greatest of all commandments, as our Father in heaven intended it to be kept.

"And, if you keep my commandments and endure to the end . . ." (D&C 14:7).

My grandmother endured to the end. She was as old as a tree; her eyes could no longer see clearly the beauties of her labor: the flowers she had planted, the winding of her old English clock, the food she had helped to preserve. Her feet no longer took her to the places she wanted to go: to the sick and the troubled, to church, and to the last resting place at the foot of the mountains, where seven of her thirteen children lay buried. But she never faltered in her desire to live the way God wanted her to live.

The Only Church That Could Help

SAMUEL H. BAILEY

The kitchen was filled with the marvelous smells of Thanksgiving dinner—roast turkey and dressing, rolls baking in the oven, and pumpkin pies. We were just about to sit down to dinner when the telephone rang. The voice at the other end of the line was filled with despair.

"Are you the Mormon church leader who works with people on the central Oregon coast?" said a woman's voice.

"I'm one of them," I assured the woman. At the time I was serving as stake president, and Lincoln County, on the coast, was part of our stake.

"I'm not a member of your church," the woman continued. "But we have a problem this morning that our church can't solve and maybe no church or organization in the world can solve. The Mormons have a reputation for being able to take care of their people any place in the world, any time. And we so need some special help this morning."

Then the words and the tears flooded forth. The woman told me that the year before, her son had married and moved with his wife to a commune on the Oregon coast. The woman and her husband had been worried about their son for months, but today they were especially concerned.

"Because it's Thanksgiving," she said, "our son called this morning to say thanks for family love and help over the years. During our conversation, we asked him about Thanksgiving dinner. He said they would not be having Thanksgiving dinner this year because they did not have any food or money and neither did the people around them.

"We live in northern California," the woman continued. "We're about ready to sit down to a lovely Thanksgiving dinner. But my husband and I are sick at heart knowing that our children are going hungry today."

She told me that she and her husband had thought about flying to Portland, renting a car, and driving to the coast to be with their son and his wife. But her son lived in too remote a spot. "We'd never be able to find them," she said. Besides, plane schedules made flying to Portland that day impossible. She and her husband had offered to telegraph some money to their son, but the small place where the young couple lived didn't have such services.

"Then we thought of the Mormon church and its reputation for caring for people under all circumstances," the woman continued. "So we called one of the local LDS leaders here in California, and he gave us your name. Can you help us?" she pleaded.

"We will try," I assured her.

"They live in the Oregon coastal mountains near a little community called Siletz," the mother said. "Do you know where that is?"

"Yes," I replied. Siletz is near Newport, where we had a strong unit of the Church. We even had some members who lived in the small town of Siletz itself—in the woods of the Coast Range mountains.

"Will you be able to find and help them, then?" she asked.

"I'm not sure we'll be able to find them. But we'll try," I promised.

I hung up and dialed the bishop of the Newport Ward. Bishop J. Charles Woods had been bishop for nearly ten years and had searched out people before—on back roads and in the tall fir forests. I knew that Bishop Woods was a man who always went the second mile. He had a few grown children of his own and would do anything he could to help.

I told Bishop Woods of my talk with the woman from northern California. He asked only one question: "How do I find them?"

I gave him the directions I had written down.

"I know where that is. I'll be on the way in a few minutes," he promised.

He needed those few minutes, it turned out, so that he and Sister Woods could pack much of their nearly ready Thanksgiving dinner into containers that went into the car, not on the table.

Within two hours, that delicious dinner had been delivered to a grateful young couple by a devoted bishop who added some words of love, encouragement, counsel, and invitation.

A few days later, a letter arrived in the mail from the woman I had talked with on the telephone. Enclosed was a check for the Newport Ward. The letter read:

"It was the reputation of the Mormons that made us think you might help feed our children in an emergency. And you did! Bless you all. We didn't have a way to solve our problem. Your church was the only organization in the world that could. We'll ever be thankful."

"Mother Is the Real Miracle"
EILEEN GIBBONS

mother, it's for you!" Three daughters who used to dash for the telephone every time it rang and answer with an anticipant "Hi!" now calmly raise it from the hook, mutter a calm "Hello," and sigh, "Mother, it's for you."

Listen closely, and you can hear them add to themselves, "It's *always* for you!"

You see, I'm one of the three daughters, and my mother is the president of a ward Relief Society. She's relatively new in the job, but during the months she has been president, we girls, our four brothers, and our father have witnessed a miracle.

Miracles aren't exactly unusual in big families. Ours has managed to remain happy through periods of economic depression, broken teenage hearts, the cruel adolescent teasings of too many freckled-faced brothers, and the mischief of a seven-year-old named Ted.

But Mother is the real miracle. For as long as we can remember, she has been doing extra, unusual things to save time, effort, and money. Rising at five o'clock in the morning to pick raspberries, midnight wall-papering parties, and the care of ten pens of rabbits are among her "saving" ideas.

Add to these washing, ironing, cleaning, and cooking for nine, and you have someone much too busy to sit and visit, read a good book, or call on a neighbor for a friendly chat. . . .

That's why when Mother told us the bishop wanted her to be president of the Relief Society we all gasped, "When?"

Mother already moved from one job to another like lightning and was the first awake and the last to bed. We'd chastised her plenty of times about moving too fast, and now the Church wanted to give her one of its biggest jobs. For several days we talked about it.

"She's just the person, but . . ."

"Wouldn't she be wonderful! But . . . ?" And then there was just the plain, "But, Mother!"

Of course Mother said yes. She had already said yes when we were going around the house wondering "When?" to ourselves and saying, "But . . ." to her.

At the time, Mother was in the Primary presidency and a teacher in the Relief Society. She was baking twelve loaves of bread every week, keeping a surplus of canned food in the basement, and frozen food in the locker.

Mother also spent an hour every day helping the child up the street improve his reading so he could be promoted. She was giving several minutes a day to Larry because he needed personal encouragement while he practiced the piano.

Torn denim knees had a way of appearing, and old rags had to be made into rugs. It was too expensive for the girls to buy all their clothes, and as long as shirts and trousers could be made from Dad's old suits and our too-small cottons, the little boys would wear them homemade.

A new latch on the door, new paint in the bedroom, the buckle torn from a shoe—myriad little jobs were already appearing daily and Mother was squeezing them in.

And now the bishop wanted her to do even more?

We girls told her how happy we were, at the same time imagining how we would probably have to quit school and our jobs so Mother could work in the Relief Society.

That was several months ago. And Mother is still busy because she still has seven children and the jobs that go along with a big family. Of course, we all have to help a little more, but the miracle is still there.

Mother has been able to do the job, keep up her home, and bring a new spirituality, enthusiasm, and happiness into her relations with her family. This is the miracle. Mother has more time and energy than she has ever had before.

"Mother, it's for you" calls her to the phone at least a dozen times every day. Someone feels she ought to let Mother know that Sister Wallace is ill. Her first counselor phones to say, "Sure, we can go visiting the shut-ins this afternoon!"

Perhaps it's a death in the ward. That usually means food to prepare, comfort to give, an assortment of needs to fill. There are flowers to arrange and children to tend.

Meetings need to be planned, work days scheduled, positions filled—the usual duties of a president. And Mother does them. . . . It is her life, her chance to serve.

She has found time to do it well, along with her washing, sewing, cooking, cleaning, and the multitude of other household jobs that come unexpectedly.

And if you tiptoe into her room almost any evening, you'll find her sitting up in bed reading a good book, the newspaper, or a magazine—to her, a luxury.

And it isn't late. Only the little boys are in bed. But you see, Mother is tired at night as always. She still has much to do, and we still tell her she does it too swiftly.

But she is a new woman. There is contentment instead of exhaustion after a day of hard work. There is joy at every chance to help or expression of gratitude from the helped. There is love between her and a hundred women she never knew before. Most of all, there is a realization and a firm testimony in her heart that wards are living, complex units that need a mother.

And the children? We enjoy our miracle Mother. And it hasn't hurt us girls at all to cook a little more often, sew on a few buttons ourselves, or even to think now and then that "he" surely would have called, if Mother hadn't been president of the Relief Society.

A Christmas Like No Other

RAY AND KLEAH NELSON

my husband, Ray, and I were awakened very early one Christmas morning to the sounds of sirens nearby. As we sleepily opened our eyes we could see a strange orange reflection on the drapes of our bedroom window. As I opened the drapes to look out and see what was happening, I could see flames and smoke coming from up the block, and to my horror I realized that our neighbor's house was on fire. We quickly put on our bathrobes and slippers and ran out of the house to see if we could help in any way.

The sight that greeted us was beyond description! The whole house was an inferno of flames, with neighbors and firemen running everywhere. We quickly found out that the family was safe, though the family cat did not make it out alive. But before the firemen were able to douse the flames, the whole house and all its contents, even the family car, were destroyed. The family had lost all of their worldly possessions, all their Christmas presents, all their hopes and dreams.

The heartsick family was taken to a nearby relative's home and my husband and I sadly returned to our home and our sleeping children, who would soon be waking, excited to unwrap their new presents. Needless to say, our Christmas celebration that year was very subdued as we explained to our children what had happened during the early morning hours. They were anxious to help and offered to share their new toys and gifts with our unfortunate neighbors. As we counseled together as a family, we realized that if our children were willing to share, probably many others would feel the same way.

After breakfast, we left ten-year-old Mike in charge and proceeded to canvass our neighborhood for blocks, asking neighbors to donate whatever they felt they could give to help this family. Everyone was generous and wanted to help. Many were shocked because they had not yet heard about the tragedy.

As we returned home to check on our children, we decided that we should reach out even farther and perhaps give the whole community a chance to participate in this worthy project. We called a few local radio stations, told them the story, and the call for help went out over the airwaves to a community just waking up to their own family Christmas celebrations.

Our home was chosen to be the collection point for the donations, and it was not long before the people began to come. All day long they came and brought money, food, clothing, bedding, household appliances, furniture—much of it new. We realized that these wonderful people were sharing their own recently opened Christmas gifts. We were especially touched as many families came with their children, who donated their brand-new toys to help someone else. By evening, hundreds of dollars had been collected and our living room, dining room, and kitchen were piled high with boxes and bags of items of every description. Even our snowy front yard was full of furniture, lawn mowers, tools, and many other items too large to fit into the house. It was truly an amazing sight.

Christmas that year is etched in our memory as a very special and unique one—one where we learned the true goodness of people and their willingness to help one another in time of need. One where the Savior's admonition to "love one another" was certainly obeyed. One where an entire community learned that the greatest joy of Christmas was not in what was received, but rather in what was given!

"When Can We Do It Again?"

ARDETH G. KAPP

Some years ago near the close of day something happened in the lives of a group of wonderful young Mia Maid girls. Prior to that afternoon, hours had been spent in cookie making, trying new recipes, program planning, writing new songs, friendship building, and lots and lots of chatting—as I recall, much more chatting than listening. Any observer would agree that was an active activity, but one might also ask, what of the principle being taught?

On the designated day all the plans for delivery of the cookies and presentations of the program were carried out as scheduled amid bubbling laughter, gaiety, and the enthusiasm of youth, everyone wanting to be a part of the action. The only flaw in the plan was that several good-sized bags of cookies were left when all the appointments had been filled. Now the question was, what to do with the extra cookies? And several suggestions came at once: "We could eat them or take them to the Scouts or sell them."

Then the voice of the class president, overriding the rest in a more thoughtful tone, said, "I know what. Let's see if there's an old folks' home where grandpas live. They wouldn't have any cookies." A call was made, an immediate appointment arranged, and a group of young girls stood at the front door of a large rest home a little less enthusiastic now about what had seemed like a great idea. The door was opened, and each girl tried awkwardly to push behind the one in front so as not to be first. There was a moment of strain with many thinking, "Why did we come?" Three of the girls quickly unloaded the sacks of cookies on the old table, which appeared to be the only piece of furniture in the room other than the beds and wheelchairs occupied by the patients.

As the girls began singing one of the songs they had prepared, in rather hushed tones and with the sweetness of youth, one or two shoulders were raised from a slumped position that had appeared to be permanent. A few patients in wheelchairs were being pushed closer by other patients. The girls continued their songs, gaining a little more courage as the warm response was evident.

At that moment a miracle was taking place. The countenances were gradually but surely changing on the faces of the aged. Expressions were changing and eyes filling with tears as the youths began a different song. This time the others hummed a familiar tune while a foreign exchange student sang the words in German. Only then did a tired, bent body slumped on the side of a bed visible through the doorway of an adjoining room raise his head and, in tone soft but audible, join in the words of his native tongue.

Heads were turned, eyes filled with tears, hearts were touched, and lives were changed. A few quiet words of appreciation were expressed, and a different group of young girls walked almost reverently down the steps of that old building. Oh, the thoughts that were shared by each during the trip home! One in an inquiring tone asked, "What happened? I've never felt like this before." And another said, almost in a whisper, "When can we do it again?" My girls and I experienced that day the message spoken of by John, "If any man will do his will, he shall know of the doctrine, whether it be of God, or whether I speak of myself" (John 7:17). For that moment we were living a principle in a Christlike way, and we all thirsted for more.

When you are in the service of your fellowmen, you are in the service of your God. We were in his service, and we felt his nearness.

A Gift for My Wife

RICHARD SIDDOWAY

We married in August and settled into a small apartment near the university where both of us went to school. We each had a year until graduation and scrimped and struggled through the autumn quarter. Now Christmas was approaching and we had little money between us to squander on Christmas gifts. We managed to put aside enough money for winter-quarter tuition and books, and that had taken all we had except for rent, utilities, and food.

We walked through the department stores of Salt Lake arm in arm with confidence of better days ahead. My bride paused before a winter coat, caressing it with her eyes and fingers. Together we looked at the price tag—seventy-five dollars. Tuition for a quarter was eighty-five dollars. We both knew the coat was out of the question. Her old coat, seam-split and stained, would have to do another year. But Christmas is a time for dreaming and hoping, and her gaze lingered long upon the coat.

When I received my paycheck on December 20, we paid what bills we owed and discovered we had twenty dollars left for Christmas. Together we found a Christmas tree lot where a stack of broken branches lay. For fifty cents they let us fill the trunk of our old car with pine boughs. We drove home and wired them together into the semblance of a Christmas tree. With a borrowed string of lights and some handmade ornaments, we created our first Christmas tree.

We agreed to spend no more than five dollars apiece in shopping for each other. While my wife drove the car to do her shopping, I walked the half dozen blocks to the Grand Central drugstore to see how far I could stretch five dollars. After considerable searching I selected a paperback novel my wife had commented about and a small box of candy. Together they came to $4.75. As I approached the checkout stand, I was met with a long line of shoppers, each trying to pay as quickly as possible and get on with the bustle of the season. No one was smiling.

I waited perhaps half an hour, and only three people were ahead of me in the line when I became aware that the line had ground to a halt. The clerk was having an animated discussion with an elderly customer. The old man was tall and thin, with an enormous shock of white hair that had been carefully parted and combed. He was wearing a pair of navy blue slacks that ended nearly three inches above his shoes. His plaid shirt was missing a button, and the sleeves of the shirt protruded two or three inches past the sleeves of his light jacket. He had an ancient leather wallet in his hand.

"Sir," barked the clerk, "the price of insulin has gone up. I'm sorry, but we have no control over that. You need four more dollars."

"But it has been the same price ever since my wife started taking it. I have no more money. She needs the medication." The man's neck was turning red and he was obviously uncomfortable with the situation. "I must have the insulin. I must."

The clerk shook her head. "I'm sorry, sir, but I have no control over the prices. You need four more dollars."

The woman immediately ahead of me in line began to mutter under her breath. She had other purchases to make and resented this clot in the artery of Christmas shopping. "Hurry up, hurry up," she whispered loudly.

"Please let me take the insulin and I will bring you back the four dollars," pleaded our elderly friend. The clerk was adamant; he had to pay before he got the medicine.

The man standing behind him put a hand on his shoulder and said, "Come on, pop, you're holding up the line. Pay the lady and let's get on with it."

"I don't have any more money," he replied. As he turned to face the man behind him, I saw his face for the first time. He had enormous bushy white eyebrows that seemed out of place on his emaciated face, but complemented the thin white moustache on his upper lip. "I've been buying insulin here for years. Always it has been the same price. Now it's four dollars more. My wife"—he threw up his hands in despair—"must have it." He turned back to the clerk.

The lady in front of me grew more agitated. The dozen or so people behind me began craning their necks to see what was holding up the line. Suddenly I stepped out of line, reached into my pocket, withdrew my wallet, and handed five dollars to the old man. "Merry Christmas," I said.

He hesitated a moment, then his blue eyes grew moist as he took the money. "God bless you, son."

I turned and walked back into the store aisles. I counted the money I had remaining in my wallet—four dollars. I replaced the box of candy on the shelf and got back into line to pay for the novel. The line moved slowly, but at last I made my purchase.

Snow was falling in soft white feathery flakes as I walked up the hill toward our apartment. The lights from the city reflected from the clouds above and gave a glow to my surroundings that matched the glow I felt inside. I turned in our driveway and saw an envelope stuck in our screen door. I removed it and found written on the front of the envelope simply, "Matthew 25:40."

I opened the door, stepped inside, and turned on the light. I ripped open the end of the envelope and withdrew a hundred-dollar bill. There was no other message. With wonder I folded the envelope and stuffed it in my pocket as I heard my wife drive in. She brought in her sack of purchases and shooed me out of our apartment while she did her wrapping.

It was only after I had driven to the department store and purchased the winter coat for my wife that I took time to get out my Bible and read the scripture written on the envelope: "Verily I say unto you, Inasmuch as ye have done it unto one of the least of these my brethren, ye have done it unto me."

To this day I have no idea who blessed our lives that Christmas.

Sources

"'You're Going to L.A.,'" by Randal A. Wright, from *Friends Forever* (Salt Lake City: Bookcraft, 1996), 148–49.

"Bakery Store Breakdown," by Mary Ellen Edmunds, from *Love Is a Verb* (Salt Lake City: Deseret Book Co., 1995), 38–41.

"Donna and Annie," by Connie Sorensen, previously unpublished.

"The Traveling Smile," by Jane Bunker Newcomb, from *Ensign,* August 1985, 67. © by Intellectual Reserve, Inc.

"An Unlikely Friendship," by Jean Davidson, previously unpublished.

"Those Who Mix the Mortar," by Ardeth G. Kapp, from *My Neighbor, My Sister, My Friend* (Salt Lake City: Deseret Book Co., 1990), 8–10.

"'Let's Put a Dollar in Each Shoe,'" by Oscar A. Kirkham, from *Say the Good Word* (Salt Lake City: Deseret Book Co., 1958), 28–29.

"Noah's Christmas Project," by Lillian Woodland, from *New Era,* December 1991, 12, 14. © by Intellectual Reserve, Inc.

"The Lord Chose Jack," by Laurel Christensen, previously unpublished.

"The Window-washing Missionary," by Linda and Richard Eyre, from *Teaching Children Charity* (Salt Lake City: Deseret Book Co., 1986), 72–73.

"The Mean Man Next Door," by Angie Olson, from *Sunshine from the Latter-day Saint Child's Soul* (Salt Lake City: Deseret Book Co., 2001), 211–12.

"'Something I Felt I Should Do,'" by Rachelle H. Jeppson, previously unpublished.

"Gifts from the Heart," by Ardeth G. Kapp, from *My Neighbor, My Sister, My Friend* (Salt Lake City: Deseret Book Co., 1990), 118–20.

"Not So Different from Me," by Patricia T. Holland, from *A Quiet Heart* (Salt Lake City: Deseret Book Co., 2000), 11–13.

"A Child's Kiss," by Carol Geil, previously unpublished.

"'My Choice Is You!'" by Mark Bybee, from *Feeling Great, Doing Right, Hanging Tough* (Salt Lake City: Bookcraft, 1991), 65–66.

"Help from the Prophet Joseph," by Margarette McIntire Burgess, from *Juvenile Instructor* 27 (1892): 66–67.

"Rachel, My Sister," by Leah Chappell, as told to Marilynne Linford, from *Ensign*, June 1987, 52–53.

"The Night I Fell in Love with My Daughter's Boyfriend," by LaRene Gaunt, previously unpublished.

"Statistics of Service," by Laurie Hansen, from "Outpouring of Love Is Inspiring," in *Deseret News*, [January] 1996.

"'I Think You Have a Fire at Your Store,'" by LaRue H. Soelberg, from *Deseret News*, December 21, 1970.

"The Great 'Bale-Out,'" by Edgar E. Eaton, from *New Era*, July 1993, 14–15. © by Intellectual Reserve, Inc.

"Special Delivery," by Shane Dixon, previously unpublished.

"'This Is All the Money I Have,'" by Ardeth G. Kapp, from *I Walk by Faith* (Salt Lake City: Deseret Book Co., 1987), 150–53.

"The Day We Picked the Beans," by Mabel Gabbott, from *Mothers in Miniature* (Salt Lake City: Bookcraft, 1976), 12–13.

"A Simple Prayer," by Beatrice D. Bullen, from *Ensign*, June 1985, 40–41. © by Intellectual Reserve, Inc.

"A Place to Call Home," by Chris Schoebinger, previously unpublished.

"A Birthday Gift for the Lord," by Spencer W. Kimball, from *Instructor*, December 1957, 360–61.

"Samaritan in Mexico," by Wendell J. Ashton, from *Instructor*, February 1955, back cover.

"Mother Fed Five Thousand," by Karen Christensen Luthy, from *Ensign*, August 1978, 64–66. © by Intellectual Reserve, Inc.

"'Take Whatever You Need,'" by Wendy McKinney, previously unpublished.

"Advice from a Pro," by Richard Eyre, from *Teaching Children Charity* (Salt Lake City: Deseret Book Co., 1986), 151.

"Five Lessons of Love," by Elaine Cannon, from *Mothering* (Salt Lake City: Bookcraft, 1993), 43–45.

"'What a Dinner We Had That Day,'" by Hannah Cornaby, from *Remarkable Stories from the Lives of Latter-day Saint Women,* 2 vols., compiled by Leon R. Hartshorn (Salt Lake City: Deseret Book Co., 1973), 2:61–62.

"The Extra Ham," by Richard Moore, previously unpublished.

"The Neighbor Plate," by Betty G. Spencer, from *Relief Society Magazine* 52, no. 7 (July 1965): 515.

"An Unsigned Note," by Mary Ellen Edmunds, from *Love Is a Verb* (Salt Lake City: Deseret Book Co., 1995), 5–6.

"Helping Hands," by Flo Whittemore, from *Relief Society Magazine* 43, no. 10 (October 1956): 673–75.

"A Visiting Teacher for Jennifer," by Cathy Blaisdell, previously unpublished.

"My Father and Blind John," by Dennis K. Allen, from *Ensign,* February 1982, 63–64. © by Intellectual Reserve, Inc.

"A Change in Routine," by Kathleen "Casey" Null, from *Where Are We Going Besides Crazy?* (Salt Lake City: Bookcraft, 1989), 57–58.

"'Here's Your Paper, Mister,'" by George Bergstrom, from "Sparks of Industry," *Instructor,* November 1968, 438–40.

"Cow for Sale," by Lynn C. Jaynes, from *Ensign,* January 1994, 59. © by Intellectual Reserve, Inc.

"'The Sky Is Blue Again,'" by Sylvia Probst Young, from *Relief Society Magazine* 55, no. 4 (April 1968): 290–91.

"He Works through His Children," by Pauline Baxter, from *Ensign,* July 1985, 51. © by Intellectual Reserve, Inc.

"Twinkle Lights," by Laurel Christensen, previously unpublished.

"The Angel Who Made the Bed," by Mark Ellison, from *Finding the Light in Deep Waters and Dark Times* (Salt Lake City: Bookcraft, 1992), 25–28.

"Heart Attack," by Ardeth G. Kapp, from *The Joy of the Journey* (Salt Lake City: Deseret Book Co., 1992), 17–19.

"Tennessee Samaritans," by David R. McKinney, previously unpublished.

"'Love, Your Visiting Teachers,'" by Melinda R. Suttner, from *Ensign,* February 1988, 54–55. © by Intellectual Reserve, Inc.

"He Still Had His Old Ones," by Michaelene P. Grassli, from *What I Have Learned from Children* (Salt Lake City: Deseret Book Co., 1993), 60.

"A Chance to Dance," by Shane Barker, from *Be the Hero of Your Own Life Story* (Salt Lake City: Bookcraft, 1994), 76–77.

"'Singing Was in My Heart,'" by Mary Johansen, from *Ensign,* December 1976, 33–34. © by Intellectual Reserve, Inc.

"The Last Room," by Jamie Gross, previously unpublished.

"Bearing One Another's Burdens," by Jill B. Brady, previously unpublished.

"Post Office Stamps," by Mary Ellen Edmunds, from *Love Is a Verb* (Salt Lake City: Deseret Book Co., 1995), 34–36.

"'Unto One of the Least of These,'" by Susan Farr-Fahncke, from *Another Ray of Sunshine for the Latter-day Saint Soul* (Salt Lake City: Bookcraft, 1999), 24–26.

"A LifeSaver in the Grand Canyon," by Jim and Carol Geil, previously unpublished.

"From the Ward, with Love," by Janet Farley Richardson, from *Ensign,* December 1985, 66–67. © by Intellectual Reserve, Inc.

"'It's a Miracle,'" by Tom Hewitson, previously unpublished.

"'There Is Room in Our Inn,'" by LaPreal Wight, from *Improvement Era* 56 (August 1953): 571.

"The Only Church That Could Help," by Samuel H. Bailey, from *Ensign,* October 1985, 69. © by Intellectual Reserve, Inc.

"'Mother Is the Real Miracle,'" by Eileen Gibbons, from *Relief Society Magazine* 41, no. 5 (May 1954): 298–99.

"A Christmas Like No Other," by Ray and Kleah Nelson, previously unpublished.

"'When Can We Do It Again?'" by Ardeth G. Kapp, from *Remarkable Stories from the Lives of Latter-day Saint Women,* 2 vols., compiled by Leon R. Hartshorn (Salt Lake City: Deseret Book Co., 1973), 2:125–27.

"A Gift for My Wife," by Richard Siddoway, from *Twelve Tales of Christmas* (Salt Lake City: Bookcraft, 1992), 43–46.